Boyd Coddington's How to Build
HOT ROD ENGINES & DRIVELINES

Motorbooks International
Publishers & Wholesalers ®

First published in 1993 by Motorbooks International Publishers & Wholesalers, PO Box 2, 729 Prospect Avenue, Osceola, WI 54020 USA

© Timothy Remus

Motorbooks International books are also available at discounts in bulk quantity for industrial or sales-promotional use. For details write to Special Sales Manager at the Publisher's address

Library of Congress Cataloging-in-Publication Data

Remus, Timothy
    Boyd Coddington's how to build hot rod engines and drivelines/Timothy Remus.
        p.   cm.
    Includes index.
    ISBN 0-87938-721-1
    1. Hot rods --Motors--Design and construction--Amateurs' manuals.
    2. Hot rods--Motors--Control systems--Design and construction--Amateurs' manuals.
    I. Title
    TL236.3.R459   1993
    629.25'04--dc20   92-43458

On the front cover: A view of the special one-off Hawk aluminum small-block for the Model A owned by Dennis Varni. *Timothy Remus*

Printed and bound in the United States of America

Contents

Acknowledgments

The list of people who contributed to this book is long, and it starts with Boyd Coddington, the man who made all of these books possible (this is number two of a four-book set). Next up is Gary Schmidt, owner of Wheeler Racing Engines in Blaine, Minnesota. Gary always seems to be down to business, moving at thirty miles per hour across the shop floor, running from one project to another. I'm sure it drove him nuts to have the work flow go all to hell whenever I showed up with my cameras and umbrellas. Well, Gary, I hope you will agree that it was all worth it.

I never could have written the chapter on fuel injection without the help of Myron Cottrell, owner and president of TPIS in Chaska, Minnesota. I'm grateful for his assistance, his knowledge, and the ride in his Corvette. Thanks also to Jim Petrykowski of Metal Fab in Minneapolis, Minnesota. Jim's a storehouse of vast amounts of information relating to hot rods, street rods, and go-fast cars of almost any type. Just down the road from Jim is Ron Quarnstrom of R&R Performance in Spring Lake Park. Ron is resident expert on dynamometers and all the useful things you can do with them.

Though our schedules didn't jive, I have to thank Art Chrisman of CARS in Santa Ana, California, for all his help and advice. It's nice when someone you've wanted to meet all your life turns out to be not only interesting and technically competent, but a gentleman as well.

Then there's John "Automatic" Sevelius from Metro Transmissions, White Bear Lake, Minnesota, a man capable of overhauling your new 700 R4 or the old Ford-O-Matic out of the '58 Edsel. John was more than willing to share his wealth of experience with me.

There are two more people to thank: Mary Lanz, my talented and lovely wife, and Jim Prokop, my designated proofreader.

Some days I think I've got the best job in the world—a job that takes me into the shops of individuals like Gary and John and Art and Myron and Jim. I spend my days (the good ones, at least) with professionals who solve problems, repair sophisticated equipment, set records, design aftermarket parts that Detroit probably thinks can't work (but do), and generally make things happen. To call this group "interesting" is an understatement. I'm always grateful not only for their courtesy and knowledge, but also for their general enthusiasm. I always seem to take a little of it with me when I leave their shop.

Introduction

This book is the second in a series of four books designed to serve as valuable reference guides for street rodders. The idea for the series came about while I was having lunch with Boyd Coddington. We were discussing at length the lack of good technical books for street rodders and hot rodders and students of the automobile. Finally, it occurred to us (Boyd probably saw it coming way before I did) that the solution to the problem was to get together and produce four new books that would serve as the "bible" to anyone who wanted to build his or her own car.

The first book spells out the fine points of chassis construction, while this book is intended to help you put a good motor between the rails of that new chassis. Whether you assemble the motor yourself or farm out most of the work, there is information here to make the job easier. The first chapter explores the possible engine choices available to the modern builder, and includes a short history of each engine family.

Subsequent chapters discuss the components needed to make a good, strong-running engine. Rather than making specific recommendations to use certain products, the approach is more generalized and geared to educating the reader. There's a lot to know before making all the decisions regarding component selection.

A fuel injection chapter is also included for anyone interested in new-tech for their street rod. But the lengthiest chapter is the one on engine assembly; I walk the reader through each step of a good engine-building sequence. It's unlikely that you will perform all these operations yourself, but you still need to know what's right and what's not, and what is worth you spending your money on.

The book also covers topics such as selecting a transmission, selecting and installing a rear axle, and finally, installing the engine and driveline. Some of the information and photos in chapter 6 on rear axles are borrowed from the first book in the series, the chassis book.

Again, the idea here is to help you build a quality new car, or renovate an existing car, and do the best job possible. I believe that the information in this book will aid you in pursuing that goal.

Recently, I received some depressing news that someone broke into a little "hunting camp" that I co-own, and trashed the place. What does this have to do with street rods? It made me think about all the senseless destruction that goes on in the world–including energy not just wasted, but running 180 degrees from the direction it could be moving. It made me reconsider the notion that when we destroy things we move backwards, and when we build and create we move ahead. Not just as individuals, but as a culture as well.

So build a car–a *really nice* car. Not just because your buddies will envy you or because it's the one you wanted to build in high school. Build it because it's the right thing to do.

Chapter 1

Choosing and Finding the Right Engine

Trying to determine which of the many available engines is the right one for your car is no easy task. First you need to decide which type of engine to run, and then which of all those small-blocks (or big-blocks or whatever) to bring home.

When determining which type of engine to run, you can always take the easy and sensible approach and run a small-block Chevrolet, probably a 350 cubic inch (ci) version. Dollars for horses, there is no better answer. But what if you

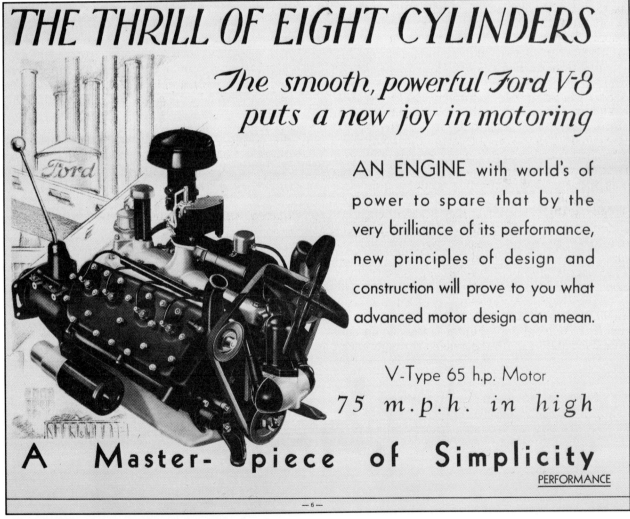

The flathead was an engineering marvel when it was introduced to the world in 1932. Today it still makes a good, durable choice for the right hot rod.

7

decide to be radical? What if you want to do something really crazy like install a Ford engine in a Ford sedan?

Ultimately, it's a matter of personal taste. If your budget is tight and there are no other overriding factors, then the small-block Chevy is the logical choice. The Chevy engine is durable, plentiful (which helps to make them affordable), and can be hopped-up more easily than any other motor.

Certain cars, however, call out for more. A nostalgia Model A roadster, for instance, might beg for a flathead while a pro-street Chevy coupe needs a blown big-block. And although it might cost more, a Plymouth coupe armed with a 426 wedge engine and two four-barrels on the old long, cross-ram manifolds (which leaves the carbs hanging out the hood sides) is hard to beat.

You need to consider your budget, the overall design of the car, and the way in which the car is going to be used. If you drive your street rod a lot, then the motor will need to be durable and achieve some kind of reasonable mileage. If, on the other hand, this new car is intended for just going down to the drive-in or running through the traps at the local drag strip, then you can trade off some of the mileage and durability.

What follows is an admittedly incomplete breakdown of the most popular street rod engines, along with some of the advantages and disadvantages of each. A complete listing would be a book in itself. The information presented here is merely a starting point, intended to get your creative juices flowing—to make you think a bit more about that all-important decision.

Chevrolet Small-Block

I've already said it—dollar for dollar there is no better value in street rod motors than the small-block Chevrolet. First manufactured in 1955 and still going strong today, this engine must rate as one of the best engine designs of all time.

A GMC blower with six "97s" really makes this 1953 flathead stand out in Rick Schnell's '40 coupe.

This Buick rod has plenty of room under the hood—but not all rods do. Careful planning will ensure that you have ample room for a neat installation with enough radiator and a good shroud.

Crate motors from Chevrolet include everything from this LT-1 shown, to more mundane Target Master 350s, both new and remanufactured.

Designed to be light, simple, and fast, the small-block was introduced in answer to the competition from Ford, Cadillac, Chrysler, and other car manufacturers that were rapidly converting to V-8 power in the early 1950s. With a total weight of just a little over 500 pounds (lb), the small-block V-8 weighed considerably less than the old six-cylinder engine.

The '55 Chevy with its new V-8 engine was an instant hit. The rocker arms were suspended on a ball, the engine was lightweight, and the bore and stroke were oversquare. These were all revolutionary design elements in 1955—though we take them for granted today. The engine has benefited from a long and fruitful evolution. Displacements of 262, 265, 283, 302, 305, 307, 327, 350, and 400ci have been produced, although for the modern street rodder, only a few of those engines make good sense.

Experienced street rod builders recommend using the 350 or 400ci small-block, especially if you're going to rebuild and upgrade the engine. The early 265, 283, and 327 engines make sense if you're doing a restoration, or if you're lucky

enough to find a bargain on a good complete engine that you intend to use as-is. The 262 and 265 engines were produced only for a few years, and are considered oddballs by most of the Chevy faithful.

The best small-block to buy is probably a 350 or possibly a 400ci. Common logic seems to suggest that the only 350 to buy is a four-bolt block. Yet, the professionals who build engines for a living claim that the four-bolt block is oversold, and that for most of us who build street rod engines with less than 400 horsepower (hp) on the dynamometer, the four-bolt is just an extra expense. These blocks definitely are stronger and they do stand up better under high-horsepower and competition use, but most of us don't really need one in our street rod.

Though all the various permutations used by Chevrolet over the years are known as small-blocks, not all of the parts can be interchanged. Early crankshafts—like those from 265 and 283 engines—had smaller bearing journals and won't interchange with those from later engines. Because the 400ci engine uses a longer stroke,

Unusual cars call for unusual engines. This little Thames panel truck carries a Fiat engine under the hood.

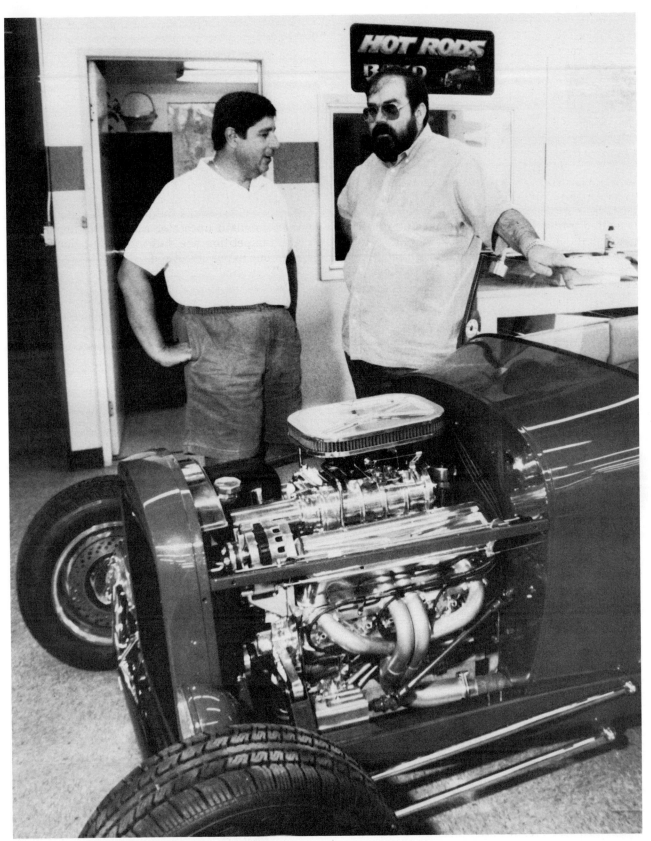

Dennis Varni and Boyd Coddington discuss Varni's Oakland-winning '29 roadster with the rather unusual small-block.

The "small-block" in Dennis Varni's roadster is a Hawk aluminum block equipped with Dart heads and a B&M blower. The valve covers, air cleaner, and oil pan were carved from aluminum by the crew at Boyd's. When it comes to choosing an engine, you're limited only by your imagination—and your budget, of course.

Seldom seen in street rods, this 351 Cleveland with single-plane intake generates some serious horsepower, although it might not make an ideal street engine.

there just isn't room on the crank for counterweights. Thus this particular engine is balanced externally, through the use of the correct damper and flywheel.

When shopping for engines, remember that those built before about 1975 did not feature flame-hardened exhaust valve seats. This means that using these heads on a modern engine probably involves spending extra money to install new exhaust valve seats. It's just one more expense and one more thing to think about as you shop the want ads.

The current high point in small-block evolution is the new, second-generation LT-1 Corvette engine. Available new from Chevrolet or from companies like Street and Performance in Mena, Arizona, this engine puts out more than 300hp on the dyno in stock trim with stock exhaust. If you buy one of these engines, remember that it is quite different from small-blocks that have gone before. No longer does water flow through the manifold, meaning new heads and new intake manifold designs. And no longer is the water pump belt-driven, meaning a new pump and a different block. The only things that interchange with earlier 350s are the crank, cam, rods, and some valvetrain parts.

The flathead evolved considerably during the twenty-one years of its production. The earliest engines, like this one, had twenty-one-stud heads. Approximate production dates can be determined by noting the number of studs, and the location of the water pumps and water outlets.

In comparing the new LT-1's measurements to those of its predecessor, the new LT-1 is 1/2in shorter, 3 1/2in lower (with new tuned port injection, or TPI, installed) 1/2in wider, and 20lb lighter. In other words, if an earlier 350 will fit, the LT-1 certainly will. Moving the alternator and other accessories higher or lower so the engine will fit in the narrow engine compartments of a street rod is easily done with aftermarket brackets. Street and Performance is one company that offers accessory brackets and an engine wiring harness that fits fuel injection requirements for this engine.

Chevrolet Big-Block

During the muscle car "wars" of the late 1960s and early 1970s, one of the more popular and potent cars on the street was the big-block Chevrolet Chevelle. Most of these models came with the 396 engine, and most proved to be damned fast when the light turned green. Since those good ol' days, the big-block Chevrolet engine has been offered in displacements of 402,

427, 454, and 502ci. (The 502 engine is a new crate engine from Chevrolet.)

One of the design criteria of the big-block Chevrolet engine was good port flow. By canting the valves, a kind of semi-hemi was produced and the designers were able to create a relatively straight port with a minimum of restrictions. This basic combination of good breathing and lots of cubic inches makes for a strong engine, one that responds well to massaging by eager hot rodders.

The extra cubes and power of a big-block have their price, however. The rat motor (as the big-block is known on the street) typically costs more than a mouse motor (the small-block) and weighs more to boot—by a good 200lb. Among the advantages of the big-block are the extra power that comes with the larger displacement, and the fact that you can create a lot of horsepower and torque while running fairly mild engine components. If you need a motor with more than adequate torque, one that will still idle around the fairgrounds all day, then the ideal compromise is a big-block Chevy engine.

There's at least one more reason to run a big block. It's that certain appeal, that down-to-business attitude that a big-block-equipped street rod exudes. Small-blocks are a dime a dozen, but when you tell 'em you've got a big-block, well, people start to pay attention.

Ford Flathead

The Ford flathead is, in some regards, the ultimate street rod engine—ultimate in a historical rather than a practical sense. A number of street rodders would like to run a flat motor, but get scared off by the flathead's poor reputation for durability. If you want a motor that will go cross-country without having to lift the hood, the answer is a small-block. If you're a reasonably good

mechanic with a keen sense of both history and adventure, then maybe the flathead is the right motor for you.

Henry Ford's first flathead was introduced to the public on March 31, 1932. We tend to look back on the venerable flathead as a very successful engine with a long history. The fact that it was indeed the first mass-produced V-8 has been lost to history.

V-8s built before the flathead were multiple castings, each block made up of two or three pieces. These were engines built in limited number and at considerable expense for cars like Cadillac and Lincoln. But Henry's problem was more than just designing a new V-8 engine. It was designing a V-8 that could be cast in one piece at the rate of hundreds of thousands per year, for a car that sold for around $550.

We've come a long way, baby. If the flathead is too old fashioned, maybe you need the ultimate in modern en- *gines—one of these ZR-1 Corvette motors with overhead cams and its own fuel injection system.*

A number of problems cropped up during the development of the flathead motor. The ignition system and lubrication and cooling systems were all trouble spots. But the biggest single problem was the casting of the one-piece block. Henry's saving grace was Ford Motor Company's leadership in foundry operations. Innovations made by Ford in their casting procedures years earlier had made mass production of the Model T possible. Now, the talents of key foundry personnel would be stretched even further to create the techniques necessary to produce the first mass-produced, one-piece V-8.

The V-8 block was a much more complex piece to cast than the old four-cylinder. While the four-cylinder used eleven cores, the new V-8 used forty-three. The design of the V-8 called for an exhaust passage that ran through the water jacket on its way to the exhaust ports. This meant a very thin casting and precise placement of those cores during the mold-making operation.

All of these problems took time to sort out. The first few batches of blocks to leave the foundry had to be scrapped. Even after the casting bugs were worked out, the early engines proved less than wonderful. The first 4,000 V-8 cars to be produced were used as demonstrators because Ford Motor Co. didn't dare sell the first models to the public.

Through persistence and constant improvements, Henry and Edsel and all the hard-working folks at the company did turn the situation around. Each year the flathead got better. During the twenty-one years of its life the flathead became a more durable, powerful, and smoother-running engine.

The V-8s produced in 1932 created 65hp. Those first flatheads used a bore of 3.0625in and a stroke of 3.750in for a displacement of 221ci. The compression ratio was 5.5:1. The water pumps were mounted to the front of each head, and the heads were bolted down with twenty-one studs.

This small-block Ford engine is equipped with the seldom seen Westlake heads, available from Gurney's American Racers.

Although it might be bigger and heavier than a small-block Chevy motor, the Chrysler hemi is in a class by itself.

15

The first major changes were made in 1937. The aluminum heads were redesigned with water outlets at the center and the water pumps moved to the upper front of the block. The Stromberg 97 carburetor was introduced that year as well, and the main bearings were converted to an insert style. In 1939, the Mercury was introduced and the flathead came in two versions. Merc engines were bored to 3.1875in, while Ford engines stayed with the 3.0625in bore. Both cars kept the 3.750in stroke for displacements of 221 and 239ci, respectively. Mercury engines had a compression ratio of 6.3:1, compared to Ford's 6.0:1 ratio. Another change came in 1939 when the flat "heads" went to twenty-four studs.

The next big change in the flathead came in 1949. In fact, engines built from 1949 to the end of the run in 1953 represent the pinnacle of flathead evolution. These last flatheads are probably the best (or at least, the easiest) type to use in your street rod.

While retaining the twenty-four-bolt pattern, the heads were changed again, with water out-

lets at the front. Other improvements included a new, more conventional, separate bell housing, and the rod bearings were changed to a non-full-floating design. The newest Mercury motors used a forged crank with a 4.0in stroke while the Ford engines received a cast crank of nodular iron and a stroke of 3.750in. The other "modern" improvement made on the last run of flatheads was the change to a conventional distributor, mounted at the front of the engine.

The final version of the flat motor is known as the BA (1946 through 1948 models are known as 59As) and is probably the easiest to match up with the correct parts. Because the BA bell housing is a separate piece, you have greater choice of transmissions that can be adapted to fit. In fact, you can get adapters to mount modern automatics like the 350 Turbo Hydro to an old flathead.

Rebuilding a flathead has been called a labor of love. If you want to make love with your flathead, be sure the machine shop you choose as partner in the project is experienced with Henry's best. A flathead isn't a complicated piece of work, but it is significantly different than

This dressed-out small-block with tuned port injection (TPI) carries all the belt-driven accessories low for a neat-looking installation.

more conventional V-8s and requires a certain "attitude"—not to mention experience—to properly overhaul.

Because these are old motors with a history of overheating, you need to worry about rust and cracks. Be sure to inspect the block (with help from an experienced flathead expert) before purchasing the motor, and be sure to have it boiled out to remove any rust and scale from the water jackets.

Ford Windsor

The little Ford V-8 was introduced in 1962, at a displacement of only 221ci. At that size, with a two-barrel carburetor it created darned little excitement. Performance enthusiasts did eventually begin to pay attention, however: first, when a small-block Ford placed second at Indianapolis in a Lotus chassis, and second, when a man named Carroll Shelby chose this little engine as the replacement for the Y-block to power a car called the Cobra.

The 221ci engine grew quickly, first to 260, then to 289, and finally to 302ci of displacement. In order to stroke the motor to 351 cubes, the new block was given a taller deck height. The larger 351ci motor received larger rod and main bearings as well.

When you suggest to a street rodder that he or she run a Ford engine instead of the venerable Chevy, three objections quickly arise: a Ford engine will cost more, it's longer than a comparable Chevy engine, and there aren't many aftermarket parts for the FoMoCo engine.

The objections are valid. But it doesn't mean that you can't run a Ford engine; it just means that for most of us, the installation of a Ford engine will cost extra in terms of both time and money.

Because Ford engines aren't as common, you will have to look farther for a good one. As mentioned later in this book, Ford engine castings don't have as much meat around their cylinders, so a 0.03in overbore is considered the limit. If you're willing to put up with a little extra hassle to run a Ford engine, then the 351 Windsor is probably the best bet for the money. With 351 cubes, the engine will make a good torquey street engine in mild trim. Another good engine option for the high-tech set is the 5.0 liter Mustang

This little billet beauty is the compact water pump built by Art Chrisman's CARS in Santa Ana, Califor- *nia, for small-block Ford engines. With this pump, the Ford is only as long as the Bow-Tie engine.*

motor, coupled to your street rod with the help of an aftermarket wiring harness.

Another drawback of the Ford Windsor cylinder heads is that they don't flow as much air as comparable Chevy heads do—even with the installation of larger valves and a good port job. The 351 heads are better, with larger valves and ports, than the earlier 289 and 302 heads.

Though there are fewer to choose from, aftermarket camshafts and intake manifolds are available. In fact, some interesting high-performance options (including complete engines) are available from Ford Motorsports, Ford's high-performance parts division.

Most of the extra length of the Ford engine is in the water pump housing. Art Chrisman's CARS in Santa Anna, California, offers a new pump that ends up making the Ford 302 engine shorter than a Chevy small-block. Remember, too, that the Ford carries its distributor at the front of the engine, so you don't need to dimple the firewall to provide clearance for the distributor.

Because most modern engines drive the oil pump via a hex shaft from the distributor, many Windsor engines have the oil sump in front—not an ideal location for most street rods. Before you start cursing or cutting the cross-member, however, note that some of the 351 engines have the sump at the rear of the pan. It's a matter of finding the right pan and oil pump pickup.

Ford Cleveland

Named after the city in which it was cast, the Ford Cleveland V-8 engine debuted in the early 1970s. Based on the "tunnel port" small-blocks developed for the Trans-Am racing circuit, the first engine in this series was the Boss 302. With canted valves, similar to a big-block Chevy, this new Boss engine came from the factory with large valves and a four-bolt block. (The first 302s had intakes of 2.23in, so large they were later reduced in size to aid low-end torque.) Enlarged to 351ci for 1971, this engine was used in everything from Mom's grocery-getter LTD to Boss Mustangs.

One of the parts you will need for that used engine is a good crankshaft. After the engine is disassembled, give the crank a visual inspection (always handle your crank with care to avoid gouged bearing journals or a bent shaft). Then be sure the engine shop Magnafluxes it before having it turned.

The hot ticket today in 351 Clevelands is the 351 HO (High Output) and the 351 CJ (Cobra Jet). These high-performance engines carry all the right stuff such as high-compression pistons and solid-lifter cams, although their large ports make them a good high-rpm motor and not a great in-town-torque motor.

Those in-the-know report that a Windsor block and crank assembly are actually stronger than the same components from a Cleveland. The *really* hot ticket in Fordland is a Windsor block mated to converted Cleveland heads, although that's probably well past the intentions and budget of most street rodders.

Though just a few pounds lighter, the Cleveland is nearly identical in size physically to its sibling Windsor V-8. But with its reputation for high performance, the Cleveland may not be as good a motor for a typical street rod as the more mundane Windsor. If you want a Ford engine, give the decision some thought before assuming one is better than the other.

Mopar Hemi—Just Say More

If street rods and hot rods started out (and in some cases remain) as race cars that never quite got to the drag strip, then they should all carry an old Chrysler hemi under the hood. Like the flathead, this is a great engine—at least from a historical perspective.

The first Chrysler Corporation hemi appeared in a 1951 Chrysler, and use of the engine was soon expanded to DeSoto and Dodge models. The hemi head's breathing ability was soon exploited by Chrysler engineers and the horsepower race of the 1950s began. In 1955, the first Chrysler 300 appeared—with a 300hp, 331ci hemi equipped with a solid-lifter cam and two Carter four-barrel carbs. In 1956 the displacement was increased to 354ci, and in 1957 that figure was bumped to the classic 392ci. Before long, the 392 hemi was the *only* engine to run in a AA Fuel dragster.

Yes, they're expensive, hard to find, heavy, and difficult to find parts for (hey, you can't have everything), but there isn't another motor quite like the old hemi. If you buy one, expect to throw

A properly built engine will have mostly new components inside when the job is finished. In addition to new bearings, timing chain, and camshaft, the engine should get new pistons and lifters. It's a good idea to lay them all out before assembly to make sure they are the right parts.

everything away except the block, crank, and heads. Find a good engine shop and then be prepared to shell out considerably more money than you would if the old round head were a small-block.

The good news is that even with modest work, these engines make a great deal of power. Internal engine parts are still available, as are external goodies like headers and intake manifolds. Some parts, like water pumps, can be exchanged for modern Chevrolet items with a little ingenuity. The old hemis can be adapted to the Chevy 350 Turbo transmission, the more modern 727 Chrysler automatic, or a nice rock-crusher four-speed (with an adapter and a Chrysler B-block bell housing).

Mopar Small-Block

This baby Mopar was born in 1964, meant to instill more power under the hood of the Dodge Dart and Valiant compact cars. Based on the old

A new oil pump doesn't cost very much, so plan to put a new one in your engine. This is a new, stock type pump from Mellings. A high-volume pump probably isn't needed for a Chevy small-block on the street, although a higher pressure spring probably is.

318, the new engine was designed to provide good power and economy in a small, lightweight package. Eventually, the displacement was increased to 318, 340, and 360ci.

The small-block Mopar is a good, durable motor. The 340 and 360ci engines were strong performers, especially those used in the high-performance Darts and Barracudas. Although these hot numbers might be hard to find, a more mundane 360 can't be too hard to find on the used market. Chrysler's Mopar performance division has recently made it easier to run one of these 360 engines with the release of their newest crate engine—a 360ci Super Commando that makes 360hp on pump gasoline. The package includes 9:1 pistons, a 284 degree camshaft, and heads with 2.02in intake and 1.60in exhaust valves.

Rebuilding one of these motors requires nothing fancy. High-performance parts are available (though harder to find than their Bow-Tie counterparts) from Direct Connection at the Chrysler Corp. If the motor you find is a 318—not to be confused with the old 318 used before about 1967—the better quality 340 and 360 high-performance parts will bolt right on.

Small-block doesn't have to mean Chevrolet. If you're running a Plymouth coupe, consider spending a little extra to keep it Mopar from one end to the other.

How Much *Is* a New Motor?

Most of us are on a budget and can only spend so much money on the motor for that new street rod we're building. Thrifty shoppers always buy used parts because they cost less than new. The logic of buying used is hard to refute—that is, until you consider some of the relative bargains offered by your local Bow-Tie dealer on new crate engines.

"Crate" is kind of a loose term. Here it means new engines offered for sale by Chevrolet (and many other General Motors Corporation) dealers. These new engines run the gamut from Target engines often used by fleet operators, to true high-performance 350s equipped with aluminum heads and intakes, guaranteed to make 345hp with a 750 Holley on top.

These new engines from GM are priced right. A Target engine (technically, Targets are Goodwrench Replacement Engines) is offered as a long-block, with heads, rocker covers, and oil pan. You need to provide the intake, water pump, fuel pump, ignition, and so on. Targets come in 305 and 350ci versions designed to replace a standard automotive, or in some cases, a medium-duty truck V-8. Suggested retail prices start at around $1,595 for a basic 350ci with four-bolt block.

At the other end of the spectrum, you'll find the complete high-performance engines offered through the *General Motors Performance Parts Catalog*. By the way, anyone who's into Chevrolets should have one of these catalogs. The list of goodies is nearly endless, featuring everything from engines to ignition systems. The current catalog lists a High Output 5.7 liter engine assembly. This is the engine with Bow-Tie aluminum heads, aluminum intake, High Energy Ignition (HEI) with the correct curve, roller hydraulic camshaft, and even a water pump. The engine comes with a twelve-month warranty with unlimited mileage, and carries a suggested retail price of $3,325.

Steve Wiberg, parts manager at Polar Chevrolet in White Bear Lake, Minnesota, explains that when it comes to complete engines, "I never get full retail, I don't think anyone does. If a person is buying a complete engine from the dealer, then they should shop around a little bit because the prices are real competitive."

If the High Output 5.7 liter seems a bit rich for your blood, on the next page of the catalog there's a 285hp 350 with cast-iron heads for only $1,995 suggested retail. Although neither of these engines may be right for you, they do provide two more options to consider in your quest for the right motor. Steve from Polar points out that there are other engines available that aren't featured in the catalog, including some remanufactured engines. Call or stop by your local Chevrolet dealer to learn more.

Finding the Right Used Engine

Whether the engine you intend to run will be another of the proverbial small-block Chevys, or something unusual like a Ford flathead, whether it is one that is rebuildable or already rebuilt (by someone reliable), or one that is brand new and

Don't be penny wise and pound foolish—spend the money to have the crankshaft assembly balanced. You will get the money back with interest in the forms of engine longevity and personal satisfaction.

in the crate, you still must go out and find that certain motor.

If you're shopping for a used motor in good (or at least rebuildable) condition, there are a number of places to pick one up. The alternatives include the junkyard, the swap meet, or the "donor car."

If you buy from a junkyard, buy only from a reputable dealer, one who will give you some kind of warranty. Maybe the dealer will guarantee that the engine will require no more than a 0.30in bore to clean up the cylinders, and that the crank can be reground to a standard undersize.

Whatever the warranty, don't buy a used engine without some assurance that the engine can be rebuilt with a minimum of trouble and expense.

Swap meets might seem like a great place to get a good deal on the engine of your dreams. The trouble is, the guy who sells you that nice clean 350 on Sunday morning is a stranger, and hard to find later if it turns out that the LT-1 you bought isn't really an LT-1.

Perhaps the best alternative when it comes to finding a good small-block Chevy or Ford engine is the concept of the donor car. Rather than buy a used engine—one you probably haven't heard run, with an unknown history—why not buy a used car instead? A beat-up Camaro or Fairlane or Impala can often be bought for less than the price of a "good" used engine.

Radical rodders sometimes go so far as to run Ford engines in Ford street rods. This shining example from

Street & Performance carries polished Ford fuel injection components. Street & Performance

There are a number of advantages to this donor car business. First, you get to hear and actually drive the engine you buy, so you have a much better idea what condition things are in. Second, in most cases you know what it is you're buying—a nice stock selection of factory parts, rather than a "mystery" engine from a swap meet. Third, the clever street rodder will use more than just the engine and transmission. Other useful parts include the steering column, the rear axle (maybe), the front brakes, the stereo, and the list goes on. The only real downside is the fact that you have to disassemble and dispose of the car when you're finished. But if you've got the right car and you're shrewd

enough, you can make enough on the remaining body and miscellaneous parts to break even on the engine.

So You've Got the Used Motor—Now What?

After buying the donor car and putting a few miles on it, you pull out the engine and set it on the garage floor. A few hours later, it's been reduced to a bare block and a few boxes of neatly labeled parts. Unless you've planned carefully for this moment you may be wondering, Now what do I do?

Actual engine assembly is covered in another chapter. But before you reach that point, you need to decide on what kind of overall approach

The small-block is always a good, logical choice for street rod power. Polished factory TPI, brackets, and *accessories from Street & Performance add a lot of sex appeal to a functional package.* Street & Performance

23

you're going to take in rebuilding the engine and in building the entire car.

Jim Petrykowski from Metal Fab in Minneapolis, Minnesota, points out that "a lot of street rodders spend more on their wheels and tires than they do on their engines. And when they do spend money on the engine, they usually spend it on the wrong stuff."

Making intelligent decisions requires that you have an overall plan for the car: How fast does it need to be? How, and how much will it will be driven? Are you planning to drive from Los Angeles to the East Coast each summer, or just cruise the fairgrounds at a few local street rod events? Is this an engine that needs to *be* fast or *look* fast? Are you aiming for good time slips (when you run at one of the Goodguys events), or good looks? If you want a really fast motor, are you willing to belly up to the bar with extra cash and extra maintenance?

Be the first kid on your block to put the new LT-1 small-block in your street rod. This polished example *from Street & Performance has special street rod accessory brackets.* Street & Performance

Jim Petrykowski has some advice, based on cars he's built and mistakes he's seen more than a few street rodders make:

"I always tell the person building the car to set a budget and then work to see how much engine they can get for that much money. A typical customer wants a small-block 350 that's snappy but doesn't cost too much and doesn't require any extra maintenance. If it's a street rodder on a budget, I tell them to budget a total of about $1,600 for the engine—that will build them a pretty nice motor if they're willing to do most of the assembly themselves.

"That allows $200 for the used engine, $800 for parts, and about $600 to machine the block and heads. The parts figure is pretty complete and includes new pistons, camshaft, lifters, valves, timing chain and gear, oil pump, and then all the miscellaneous things like the rings, bearings, and gaskets."

So here's a quick worksheet of what you might want to consider budgeting:

Used engine	$200
Parts	$800
Machine work	$600
Total	$1,600

Jim continues: "Some of my customers think that the total figure is OK, but they want to skimp on the engine work and then spend that money on things like an aluminum intake and a new Holley carburetor. I'd rather see them build a real quality engine—if money's tight they can always add the new intake and carburetor later.

"I tell 'em to find a good engine shop and then work with the guy who runs that shop.

Don't try to weasel the guy out of every nickel. Let the engine shop do what they do best, follow their advice for the kind of engine you want to have—and then save some money by assembling the engine yourself.

"Too many street rodders will skip having the engine balanced and spend that money on a new carburetor. They should spend the money building a good solid engine; they can always change the carb later. Besides, a rebuilt Quadrajet will perform just fine for most rodders because they really don't push the cars all that hard anyway. It seems like people are painting more and more engine parts, so a guy can just paint the stock intake manifold and run the old carb [have it rebuilt] and spend that $500 more wisely.

"And if really good performance is what a rodder wants, they get more performance per dollar from a set of lower gears or a higher stall converter or maybe a nitrous setup than they do by spending that same amount of money on high-tech engine parts."

Jim adds: "I can't stress it enough that they should do some research, pick a good engine shop, and then treat that shop like a partner in the project. Ask for advice. If big horsepower is what you've just got to have, then ask for their advice on how to get it. A strong engine is a combination of parts that work together. The headers need to work along with the cam, the head, and the carburetor. You can't just buy whatever is on sale or the parts that are most popular with your friends. You need a package of parts that work together."

Chapter 2

Choosing and Testing Engine Components

Finding the "right stuff" is never easy because most of us don't know what it is. This chapter is intended to aid the street rodder in his or her quest for engine goodies. Deciding which one among hundreds of intake manifolds, for example, is best for your small-block Chevy is a tall order. Thus, the approach that I am taking here is to look at the right types of equipment—such as manifolds, camshafts and such—for your vehicle, and then offer guidelines for selecting them instead of specific recommendations.

Some of the information was obtained from interviews with various professionals while other details, like those presented in the cylinder head section, are simply listings of the commonly available hardware.

The *real* goals of this chapter are to make you a better consumer, and give you a better understanding of how an engine works, and an appreciation for good torquey motors that work at the rpm ranges commonly used on the street. It's easy to spend your money on those fancy parts in the catalogs and magazines. It's much harder to spend that money wisely and get a good return in performance.

There are a few key things to keep in mind as you ponder the many expensive options available—each one better than the one before—that you might bolt onto this shiny new engine.

First, remember the words of that wise old mechanic who said: "People forget that everything you bolt on that engine, from the air cleaner to the carburetor to the heads, the cam and the headers, must work together. Each of those parts affects all the other parts."

Second, just because everybody else on the block is using a particular carburetor or intake manifold doesn't necessarily mean that *you* should.

Design your engine as a package with each part carefully chosen to work with all the other parts. Remember that one particular carb or intake isn't better than another in *all* situations. One part might work better in your situation in conjunction with all the other parts that you intend to use. Before making your parts selections, get the input of some experts who know more than you do. If a quality engine building shop is doing your machining and some of the assembly work, ask their help in choosing parts that will give the kind of torque and horsepower curves best suited to your car and your driving style.

If you read the interviews in this book, you will find a few points that all these professionals

This Sunnen valve machine in the Wheeler Racing Engines shop can be used to "grind" the valve seats, as well as cut out and install new seats.

agree on when it comes to building a good street engine.

Starting at the top, most of the experts felt that 650 cubic feet per minute (cfm) is as much carburetor as a street engine can use. Jeff Fiala from Wheeler Racing Engines in Blaine, Minnesota, tells of having a moderately built-up 350 in a Camaro and access to two Holley carburetors, a 650 and a 750. He said the difference in going from the 750 to the 650 was profound: "I just couldn't believe it, the car seemed so much faster with the 650 on it. With the 650, when I gave it gas the car really jumped."

Underneath the carburetor, the consensus is for a dual-plane manifold. With this design, the intake pulses are separated from one another by 180 crankshaft degrees. Looked at another way, as you go down the firing order, every other cylinder in the firing order draws off one side of the carburetor. The first cylinder in the firing order might draw off the right side, then the second will draw off the left side, and the third will draw off the right side again. By separating the intake pulses there is better flow in the manifold at low speed and better low-rpm operation. Each

intake pulse and firing is separated from the next by 180 crankshaft degrees. The alternative is a single-plane manifold, where all eight runners converge in one big open plenum under the carburetor. These work well at high rpm, but not very well on the street.

Another area of consensus is the camshaft and its specifications. The tendency is to get too carried away and install a stick with nearly 300 degrees of duration and more than 0.5in of lift. Those in-the-know recommend a lot less than that, and remind potential buyers and engine builders that less is more—more low-speed torque with camshafts of reasonable duration.

Picking the Right Cylinder Heads

Including a cylinder head section in a street rod book might seem like it's more information than the average street rodder needs (which is better than the reverse). Yet, anyone who wants to build a good, durable, powerful engine will have to give some serious thought to the heads that are used. Unlike a carburetor, bolting on a different set of heads is more than a little work and not the kind of thing you want to be doing

The valve machine is set up to cut out the old, non-hardened exhaust seat so a new one can be installed.

over and over every weekend. Better to get it right the first time.

An engine is, after all, only an air pump: more air in means more power out. Achieving high-performance, however, is not just a matter of using big carburetors or high-lift camshafts. The air leaving the carb must move through the ports in the cylinder head before it reaches the valves. In most engines, the single greatest restriction to airflow is found in the cylinder heads. While a larger carb can be bolted on with ease, a larger cylinder head is much harder to bolt on.

Given these facts, it seems only fair that you spend a little time considering which head to run on your street stomper and how best to prepare that head. The idea is not to make you the most skilled Dremel-tool operator on your block, but

rather to make you a more informed consumer. So when you go out looking for that set of heads that's "just right", you will know what to buy.

Just a reminder, the emphasis here is on street engines for street rods, and the heads and porting techniques described are viewed from that perspective—not from that of the drag strip or the oval track.

First, we will deal with the various heads available for the more popular engines. Then we'll explain the techniques that can and should be used to improve their performance.

Small-Block Chevrolet Heads

Since its introduction, the small-block Chevrolet engine has seen literally hundreds of

This is not a before and after picture, but rather a comparison between a stock Chevy casting and one that has been pocket ported.

28

different head designs. Of this confusing array, many can be disregarded as options due to their age and the fact that you are unlikely to find them in the junkyard or at the swap meet.

When you start your quest, remember that valve size isn't everything. Also, in some parts of the country, the supply of the most desirable original equipment manufacturer (OEM) heads is quite limited, so it may end up being cheaper and easier to buy an aftermarket head.

As Gary Schmidt, owner of Wheeler Racing Engines, explains: "A lot of times, the customer brings in two heads, we clean them, and then find that one is cracked. Well, then the guy has to go out and find another head—sometimes you can only buy a set. So what we often see is people who have to buy three or four heads to get two really good ones."

So shop carefully and try to buy used heads on the condition that you can get your money back if they turn out to be cracked. The various OEM heads are identified by their casting numbers. Most students of the small-block shorten

the seven-digit number and use only the last three digits.

Buying the definitive heads for your small-block means more than just finding the right heads in good condition. Some of the large-valve heads won't work on 305 engines due to interference between the valve and the cylinder at maximum lift. A second problem is the difference in combustion chamber volume (the more common castings have volumes of either 66 or 76 cubic centimeters, or cc) and the effect that volume has on the compression ratio.

If you're using a set of heads different from the stock castings (or swapping 350 heads onto a 305), be sure to check with the engine shop doing the machine work so that you end up with the desired compression ratio. The last thing to check is the accessory bolt holes on the end of the heads to ensure that accessories such as your air conditioning compressor, for example, can be bolted on.

In the mid-1970s, Chevrolet cylinder heads changed in at least two significant ways. This is

These two closeups show the difference in size between a stock head with 1.94in intake valves and one that has been opened to accept a 2.02in valve.

You can see how much bigger the reworked port really is.

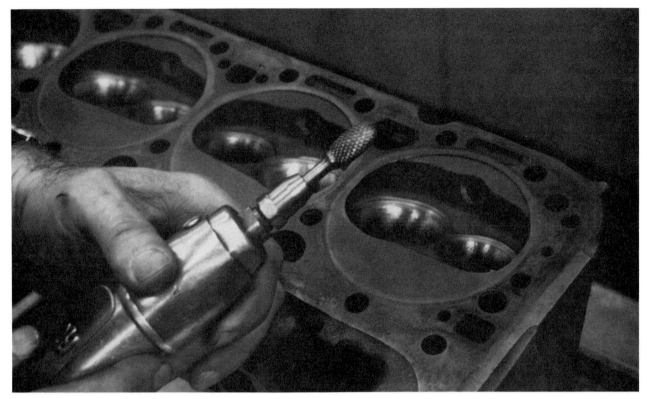

Most of the porting work is done with this 5/8in carbide bit that is about 2.5in long.

A look down into a stock intake and exhaust port. Note the sharp edges where the area below the valve meets the port in the cylinder head.

one of those good news–bad news deals. The good news is that the heads produced after that period carry flame-hardened exhaust valve seats to accommodate unleaded gas. If you're in doubt about which seats should or shouldn't be used, be sure to ask the shop doing the valve and port work. New seats can always be pressed in later, but it adds extra costs to the project.

The bad news about the cylinder head revisions is that while the seats got better, the head castings got worse. Heads manufactured after about 1975 have much thinner castings—and they sometimes can't be machined to correct a warped condition. These heads are also more prone to cracking during their service life.

And finally, the casting numbers, please. Following is a list of casting numbers for cylinder heads made for various Chevrolet small-block V-8 engines:

461: This is the original "fuelie head" used on fuel-injected Corvettes during the early and mid-1960s. It is also the original carrier of the much-talked-about double-hump casting mark. The head came in at least two variations, with different combustion chamber volumes. The 461 is still considered to be a pretty good head for the street—*if* you can find a set in reasonable condition.

462: Produced during the late 1960s, the 462 is another casting marked with the Camel logo. The head is similar to its numeric predecessors in both shape and function. The subtle differences between the 461 and 462 include a change in the location of the spark plug and the shape of

Art Chrisman: Living Legend

Art Chrisman, owner of CARS in Santa Ana, California, is a name we've all heard of. A visit to his shop proved very instructive. Though Art is a living legend in the hot rod business, a look around his busy shop will show the visitor that Art is one legend who has very little time to rest on his laurels.

The shop is filled with a variety of projects, everything from a flathead-powered '34 Ford with nearly stock running gear and body dimensions, to a long dragster chassis being fabricated over against one wall. Art is known for his engine work, and the engine room contains a number of projects. A small-block Ford engine with special Westlake heads and a short CARS water pump waits for key parts. Along the opposite wall sit flatheads, hemis, and big-block Chevy engines. Above the engines are three *Hot Rod* magazine covers, framed and under glass. The dates span six years, and each cover features an Art Chrisman car.

The first time Art was honored by *Hot Rod* for his innovation was May of 1953, and the last time was in 1959 when Art's full-bodied Chrysler-powered *Hustler* dragster graced the cover.

In fact, *Hustler* still survives. When I stopped by on a Monday for this interview, Art had been out over the weekend with the dragster. He hadn't been showing the car, he had been running it—running it past 180mph. Not bad for a guy who started collecting trophies in the early 1950s.

Q: *When people modify their engines for more power, what are some of the common mistakes they make?*

Art: Well, if I had to pick just a few things, I would have to pick cam timing and compression. Everyone assumes that when you line the gears up on the stock marks the timing is OK. Sometimes it is, sometimes it isn't. They should always check the actual timing with a degree wheel and compare it to the specifications that come with a new camshaft.

The other thing is compression. Some of these guys don't have equipment to "cc" the heads [determine the actual volume of the combustion chamber in cubic centimeters], so they don't know what the compression ratio is. They rely on the piston manufacturer for the ratio. But if you buy a piston that's 10:1, it's 10:1—as long as you use the right head. They should find out what the cc of the head is and then find out how that affects the compression.

Another thing on the street is the ignition timing. To get mileage on the highway you need a vacuum advance. But you want to get the ignition advance curve set on the machine so the advance follows the engine's needs. People shouldn't stray too far from the way the timing is set up coming from Detroit.

Q: *You said ignition timing isn't as accurate as people think it is. Explain what you mean?*

Art: People think that if the engine's out of time they can compensate by moving the distributor. They don't understand that if the cam is off ten degrees they can't compensate by moving the ignition timing. It comes back to making sure the cam is installed correctly.

A good double-check during the assembly is to make sure that when the number one piston is at TDC [top dead center] that a straightedge run across the two cam lobes [for number one cylinder] is perfectly straight [this assumes a single-pattern cam].

Q: *Do people buy the wrong parts for a certain situation? Are they still buying too much carburetor for the street?*

Art: Yes, they still buy too much carb. A street 350 only needs 600 or 650cfm, but the guys are putting 800 and 850 double-pumper carbs on their street engines and it's just too much—it hurts the driveability. Bigger isn't always better. Overcamming and overcarbing are the two biggest things that people do—it makes for a non-fun kind of street car.

Surrounded by current projects and past glory, Art Chrisman of CARS remains a very active hot rodder.

Q: *How does a person do a better job of choosing a good set of performance modifications? For example, how does Mr. or Ms. Average pick a good set of components—a cam, carb, and exhaust—that will work together to make a good strong street engine?*

Art: It's pretty hard—unless you have the experience. I like to build and drive real dependable, usable engines. To do that you can't run a big carb and a lot of cam and a single-plane manifold. You need a two-plane manifold, a medium cam that isn't too radical, and a 650cfm carb. Those are the rules of thumb that I discovered years ago. These days the gas is so bad that you've got to keep the compression down. Pump gas is about ninety-two octane, and you can run 9.0:1 or 9.2:1. Otherwise, you need an additive or race gas.

Q: *What kind of cam specs do you look for in a street 350?*

Art: Around 260 or 270 degrees of duration is plenty (at 0.050in of lift). Lift shouldn't go over 0.500in. Don't put too much spring on the valve. In most cases on the street you can run hydraulic lifters; they rev to 6000rpm without any floating problem. That makes it easier to work on and quieter. We take an LS6 engine that you buy from Chevrolet and we pull out the solid-lifter cam and install a hydraulic cam and put in hydraulic lifters and lower the compression and still run ninety-two octane gas. They run like Jack the bear and pull 440hp on the dyno.

Q: *The magazines are full of rocker arm articles and ads. How important is all of this on the street?*

Art: On the Chevys I always use 1.5:1 rockers, it's always worked for me. I put a lot of needle bearing rockers on, like the ones from Crane, and on the street that setup seems to work pretty well on the Chevys.

People get in trouble because they don't use good enough parts. I always tell people to buy the very best parts they can afford. A few years ago we built an engine for a guy to use at Bonneville, and we used the very best components we could find. Well, he ran that engine for five or six years. He ran it and ran it and it never gave him any trouble. He pulled it apart in the winter and inspected all the parts, you know, but that was all he ever did. People should buy the best parts they can, the highest quality parts they can afford.

Q: *There are a lot of ads for preassembled short blocks sold mail order. Are they good engines?*

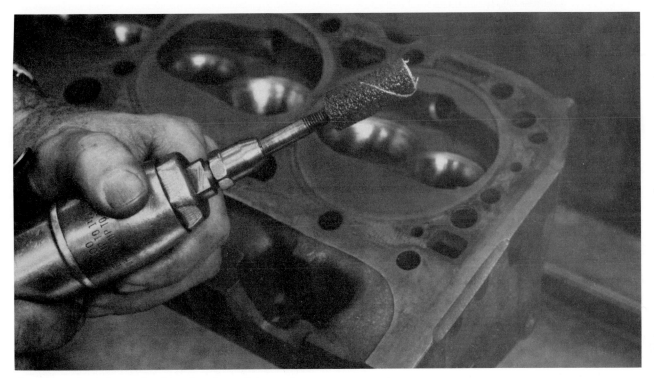

Another tool of the trade, this abrasive roll is used to finish the inside of the ports after the metal has been removed with the carbide bit.

Gary finishes the pocket-port job with the abrasive roll.

mance and is still available new from your local Chevy dealer.

292: The 292 head is an evolutionary improvement over the 492 casting, with a different spark plug location, more meat under the valve spring pads, and no exhaust heat crossover passage. The 292 is commonly referred to as a "turbo" head.

624: This head was used from the late 1970s up through the mid-1980s. Although most were equipped with 1.94in intakes and 1.50in exhausts, some L82 Corvettes used the 624 heads with larger, 2.02in and 1.60in valves.

882: The 882 head was used during the late 1970s and features flame-hardened exhaust seats. Some came with small, 1.72in intakes (rather than the more common 1.94in dimension), but all carried the 1.50in exhaust. Both the 624 and the 882 are currently quite common in junkyards and at swap meets.

993: Though some would disregard this head because it is an open-chamber design rather than the superior closed chamber, the 993 is often used to good advantage on the street. In fact, the engine built by Wheeler Racing Engines as a demonstration project carried a set of 993 heads and produced almost 400 horses.

487: The 487 is very closely related (some would say nearly identical) to the 993 casting from the early 1970s.

Cast-iron Bow-Tie heads: Introduced in about 1980, the Bow-Tie heads were designed for high performance from the start. The ports are big—in fact, not everyone thinks these are a good street application—so be sure to consult with your engine guru before bolting them onto your street rod engine.

Aftermarket heads: Due to the popularity of the small-block, a wide variety of aftermarket heads are available. Of these heads, however, only a few are designed to replace their factory counterparts in street applications. The most popular aftermarket head for the street is the Dart SR (Street Replacement) head. These castings are designed to replace the popular Chevrolet castings such as those already listed, at a reasonable cost.

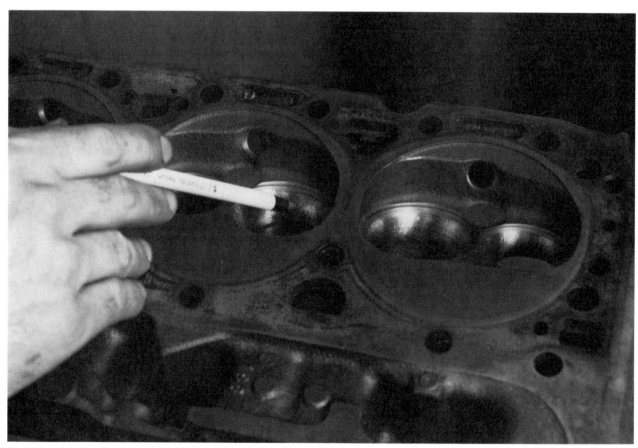

The idea is to enlarge and blend the area under the valve seats—the most restrictive area on street engines with mild camshafts.

As the supply of "good" factory castings dries up, more and more enthusiasts are using Dart (also known as World Products) heads. They claim that these heads don't flow quite as much air as the Chevy castings after a pocket-port job, but that might be because the shops doing the porting don't have fifteen years of experience with these relatively new castings. Dart also offers a high-performance head in cast iron, available with different plug locations and combustion chamber volumes.

Chevrolet Big-Block Heads

Like the small-block, this engine has been produced with a number of different head castings. The various cast-iron heads fall into two basic categories, oval port and square port.

The designers at Chevrolet did their homework when they developed this head, at least with regard to airflow. All the big-block heads flow pretty well; in fact, the square-port heads flow so much air they are not recommended for street applications. A better choice is the oval-port heads, available in a number of different configurations.

The most popular big-block castings from Chevrolet are the 049 and the 781. Although the stock 781 flows a bit more air, the airflow evens out when comparing a ported 781 to a ported 049.

Part of a good pocket-port job is to back-cut the valve to eliminate more restrictions in the path of the air-fuel mixture.

This closeup shows how the area under the valves (on a different head) has been enlarged and blended with the port.

Rick from Ron Quarnstrom's shop (R&R Performance) works with the seat grinder at the end of a porting job. Rick reports that to do two used small-block heads, a good pocket-port and valve job often takes him nine to twelve hours.

Ford Windsor Heads

Windsor series engines include displacements of 260, 289, 302, and 351ci. As the displacement increases, the valves get bigger, so no matter what the displacement, use the 351 castings. Art Chrisman says that he ports the 351 heads and installs Chevy 2.02in intake and 1.60in exhaust valves. He says they may not flow quite as much air as a good pair of Chevy heads, but they're close.

If close isn't good enough, Dart offers a high-performance cast-iron head with better port shapes than the stock offerings. Some other alternatives include aluminum heads from Ford SVO, or you can convert Boss 302 or 351 Cleveland heads, though this last option gets to be a fair amount of work and expense.

Ford Cleveland Heads

The Cleveland engine is known as a "breather." Like the big-block Chevy, this engine uses canted valves to help create less restrictive intake and exhaust port shapes. This is another case where you can have too much of a good thing. When the ports and valves get too big, it hurts air velocity at low engine speeds. The result may be great horsepower figures at high rpm, but poor torque production at lower rpm.

The Cleveland heads came in various forms, the four-barrel heads having the largest ports. In

Rocker arms come in various styles, from stock type to full roller. The demonstration engine used the rockers on the bottom—heavy-duty stock type rockers (with

stock 5:1 ratio) with a longer slot to accommodate a higher lift cam.

a street engine, the two-barrel heads with smaller ports might actually do a better job of making good low-speed torque. Like some of the Chevy castings, they came with different combustion chamber volumes so if you switch heads, make sure you get the desired compression ratio.

Small-Block Mopar Heads

One of the best small-block Mopar heads used by the factory came on 1968-1971 high-performance 340 engines. These engines have 2.02 and 1.60in intake and exhaust, and carry a casting number of 894. Later model 340 heads from the early 1970s carry the same large valves and rate as a "next best" option (with a casting number of 915). Moving down the desirability list are the later 360 heads, some of which have an intake valve of 1.88in. Note, however, that these intake seats can be opened to the 2.02in dimension.

By comparison, the 318ci heads have smaller valves and smaller ports and runners. So if it's horsepower you want, then take the time to find either 360 or 340 heads.

The Art of Reconditioning Cylinder Heads

The heads you bolt onto your engine, be it a small-block or an old hemi, should be treated to a little TLC to bring their performance back to at least like-new condition. Not all of us are not going to do our own valve job or porting work, but we should understand the importance of having a good valve job done and the gains in airflow that accompany a little smoothing of those ports.

Reconditioning a set of heads starts with disassembly, cleaning, and checking for cracks. Some cracks, near the seats for example, can be seen visually after a good cleaning. Others won't show up, except under the special lights of the Magnaflux machine.

If the heads pass the crack test, then reconditioning can proceed. Some things to keep in mind are the flatness of the sealing surface, the condition of the guides, and the condition of the valves themselves.

Most heads can be planed flat if the sealing surface isn't perfectly flat. Valve guides on a well-worn set of heads will often need some kind of attention. Failure to replace or recondition the

The demonstration heads have been tapped for screw-in rocker studs. The lifters are anti-pump-up and the pushrods are stock.

guides can lead to oil burning and a short-lived valve job. If the wear on the guides isn't too bad, then they can be knurled instead of being replaced. The knurling raises metal on the inside of the existing guide, which is then reamed to the correct size for the new or used valve stem. Guides worn too badly for knurling are replaced by new guides available in a variety of materials.

The valve job can commence following guide installation or repair. Be aware that not all valve jobs are created equal, however; the job done at the local parts store is seldom the same three-angle valve job done at a good high-performance shop. The next step is to do a pocket-port job after the three-angle valve job. (More on pocket porting in a minute.)

The essential duty of a valve and seat is to open, allowing the mixture in or out, and then to close and seal perfectly against the very high pressure generated inside the cylinder. A basic valve job, if done well, will allow the valves to accomplish these goals.

The Value of Dyno Testing

In order to explore this idea of dyno testing further I contacted Ron Quarnstrom, owner of R&R Performance located in Spring Lake Park, Minnesota. Ron has run this dyno facility for six years and tested more than 1,000 motors.

Q: *Ron, when you rent the dyno to other people to use, how much does the basic rental cost, and how long does it take?*

Ron: The basic package is a four-hour rental and it costs $185. That four hours includes hookup time. If it's a small-block, then everything hooks up pretty easily. Additional time is sold at $42.50 per hour.

Q: *Is four hours enough time to check out a recently built motor?*

Ron: Yes, that usually leaves enough time to do the initial break-in, check for leaks, and do enough full-power and cruise tests to get everything working the way it should be.

Q: *Do you do more during that four hours than just full-power pulls?*

Ron: Yes, if the guy tells me the motor is for a street car or a street and strip car, then I figure it's going to spend most of its time on the highway just cruising. So I like to run the motor at around 2600rpm—or whatever his cruise rpm will be—and then put gradually increased loads on the engine. It takes about thirty horses to push a typical car down a level road at 60mph. I start with a thirty-horse load and increase it in 30hp increments until I've got full throttle. This would simulate everything from a small hill to a passing situation.

Q: *What kind of air-fuel ratios do you like to see during the cruise test?*

Ron: I want the ratio with a light load to be near the ideal of 14.7:1. That will give the owner maximum economy during light-throttle cruising. As the load increases, the air-fuel ratio should gradually increase to a maximum power ratio, something between 12.8:1 and 13.2:1. The light load fuel ratio can be adjusted with the main jets in the primary side of the carb, but any dip in the ratio as the load increases can be corrected with a different power valve.

Q: *Based on what you've seen run on the dyno, do you feel people need to spend tons of money on high-performance parts in order to get good performance?*

Ron: No, they don't. My daughter and I built a motor for her Camaro and we did it without all the fancy parts and that engine works great. We started with a 400ci small-block, we used cast pistons and a cast crank and stock rods with new bolts. The cam is a real mild hydraulic grind. The engine produces a maximum of 477lb-ft of torque at 3750rpm and 409hp at 4750rpm. This is a fairly mild motor. The carb is a stock Quadrajet, the intake is a Performer from Edelbrock with the EGR hooked up. The secret is the heads. I ported those heads to reach maximum flow at 0.400in of valve lift.

Q: *How does all this work on the street?*

Ron: It gets 17.8mpg and still turns 13.19 second ETs at the strip. The strip time was with a stock converter and the automatic shifting at only 4750rpm. I think that if we change the shift point and maybe feed the carburetor fresh air from outside the engine compartment, that we can get it down into the high twelves. That's darned good for a car that gets pretty good mileage.

Q: *In all these years of dyno testing motors, you must have seen a lot of mistakes. What are the mistakes people most commonly make when they build a motor for the street?*

Ron: I see a lot of engines with poor idle quality. Sometimes it's too much camshaft and sometimes it's a vacuum leak between the intake manifold and the heads. Remember, a lot of these people are putting on aluminum intakes and they don't always fit right. I go through a series of checks—sometimes using one of my own carburetors—in order to decide if the poor idle quality is the cam, a bad carb, or a vacuum leak.

I also see people use camshafts with too much duration and they put too much emphasis on horsepower and not enough on torque. If the transmission is an automatic, when you pull away from the light the motor might be turning only 2000rpm. Now if you mash the pedal, a lot of those motors just bog down because they aren't turning fast enough for the cam and all the other parts to work. With a good torque motor, there's lots of power way down low in the rpm range and it makes a better all-around street car.

Dyno Test Demonstration on Small-Block Chevrolet Engine

Test	200rpm/sec acceleration
Vapor pressure	0.38
Displacement	355ci
Test number	1
Fuel specific gravity	0.715
Barometric press.	29.35
Stroke	3.480in

Speed	CB torque	CB power	Air-fuel ratio
(rpm)	(lb-ft)	(hp)	
2500	321	152	12.3
3000	339	193	12.2
3500	343	228	12.6
4000	357	272	13.0
4500	372	319	13.0
5000	366	348	12.2
5500	348	364	12.4

Test	200rpm/sec acceleration
Vapor pressure	0.38
Displacement	355ci
Test number	5
Fuel specific gravity	0.715
Barometric press.	29.35
Stroke	3.480in

Speed	CB torque	CBpower	Air-fuel ratio
(rpm)	(lb-ft)	(hp)	
2500	334	159	11.1
3000	350	200	12.3
3500	357	238	11.7
4000	380	289	12.3
4500	398	341	12.1
5000	389	370	12.4
5500	373	391	12.2
6000	343	392	12.9

These abbreviated copies of dyno printouts show test results of the demonstration engine assembled in chapter 4. The motor is probably a little strong for a typical street rod. The compression is 9.5:1, the cam specs are 234 degrees duration for the intake and 244 degrees for the exhaust, and lift is 0.450in and 0.510in, intake and exhaust. The manifold is an Edelbrock Performer and the carb is a 750 Holley (a 650 would work better on the street). The heads have been massaged as well. But it does make horsepower! Nearly 400 corrected horsepower on pump gasoline.

The difference between run number one and number five is a few more degrees of timing (thirty-eight degrees total), a 1in spacer under the carburetor, and probably a few horses just because the engine loosened up from one run to another.

These were full-power acceleration tests run on a tight time schedule. If you have your street rod engine run on the dyno, be sure the operator does some cruise testing as well as the full-power pulls. Careful cruise testing (see Ron Quarnstrom's comments for more on dyno runs for street engines) will ensure that the engine gets good mileage and produces maximum horsepower.

There are added criteria in high-performance engines. These engines require more than just an open-and-shut valve that seals correctly. The valve and port, when open, must flow as much air as possible. As delivered from the factory, most castings feature ports that are in less than optimum condition for airflow.

Since the beginning of automotive time we've heard the word ported (or "ported and relieved" from the Beach Boys' *Little Deuce Coupe*). In recent years, the term pocket port has been heard on the street. So what do these terms mean?

As David Vizard points out in his excellent book *How to Build and Modify Chevrolet Small-Block V-8 Cylinder Heads,* the valves in most engines, especially street engines with less than radical cam profiles, are open less than halfway a high percentage of the time. Thus, the air or exhaust is often forced to snake its way between a partially open valve and its seat.

Rodders often concentrate on the port near the intake manifold or where it exits to the exhaust manifold. Yet, the greatest restriction to airflow during the majority of time the engine operates is between the valve and its seat. What this means is that on a port job done for street use, the most important area is the one closest to the valve seat, and the backside of the valve itself.

The intention here is not to teach you *how* to port your own heads, but rather to convince you to do some research before you try. If you hire out the work, be sure that the porting professional who does the work understands that this is a street engine—with different needs and different porting criteria than a full-race engine.

What We Can Learn at the Dyno School

Everyday, we read articles in popular automotive magazines describing this dyno run or that dyno run. Charts and graphs and eight-by-ten glossies describe in detail how the engine in question put out eight zillion horsepower at 9200rpm. That may be all well and good, but the full capability of a dynamometer is never satisfactorily explained.

In addition to measuring peak power, the dyno can be used to do the initial engine break-in, evaluate basic engine operation following a rebuild, determine the type of torque and horsepower curves that a particular combination of parts achieve, and allow the technician to do some sophisticated fine-tuning of the engine prior to installing it in the car.

The engine that is described here is the same 350 Chevrolet demonstration engine used in chapter 4. Jeff Fiala from Wheeler Racing Engines is the technician, the same man who did most of the engine assembly. The testing took place on a Super Flow 901 at Anoka Ramsey Sports Center in Anoka, Minnesota. What follows is a blow-by-blow account of this particular dyno run, with some added comments regarding

the value of a dyno run like this one for the typical street rod engine.

First, everything had to be hooked up: the water, wiring, and the electrical system. Then it was time to fire the engine. Once the carburetor had gas, the engine fired, and Dave Harlander, the man in charge of the dyno at Anoka Ramsey Sports Center, ran the motor up over 2000rpm. He explained that cam break-in is critical during the first few minutes of running. The cam lobes are lubricated by oil that is splashed up from the crankshaft, so it is important to keep the engine speed up over 2000rpm for the first twenty minutes of running.

During this time, basic engine operation is closely observed: Are there any external leaks? Is the temperature OK? Are all eight cylinders firing? It's easy to make a little mistake when assembling an engine, and it's a lot easier to fix that oil leak or loose bolt now instead of waiting until the engine is installed in the car.

Dave Harlander of Anoka Ramsey Sports Center sets up the demonstration engine on the dynamometer.

Most engine builders recommend a dual-plane intake manifold like the one on the bottom for street use. A single-plane manifold at the top is just one big plenum attached to eight runners.

After the motor had run for twenty minutes, Dave ran the revs a little higher and put a light load on the engine just to see how everything felt. When he and Jeff were satisfied with the engine's operation so far, they decided that it was time for the first pull to full power.

Dave set the rate of acceleration on the Super Flow control board and after a quick double-check of all the gauges, he opened the throttle all the way. The engine picked up speed but in a controlled fashion, as the dyno increases the load at each "step" in the rpm range. As the digital tachometer soared past 4000rpm the engine really started to sing—and a deep roar came through the brick wall and the reinforced glass window.

The first test was shut down at 5500rpm and suddenly it seemed very quiet. Everyone looked at the computer screen to check the numbers, and Dave punched a button and the printer started to chatter as all the data was recorded on paper.

Though everyone wanted to see what kind of power the engine made, the first run was used

mostly to ensure that everything was dialed in. In other words, what are the air-fuel ratios throughout the rpm range? When is the vacuum secondary on the Holley carb coming in? How do the temperature and oil pressures look? and so on.

The only problem that could be found on the Chevrolet 350 was a reluctance of the secondary to open. The Super Flow setup has two gas feed lines, A and B. The A line runs to the primary float bowl and the B line to the secondary float bowl. Both lines are monitored and can be printed out as pounds per hour at any rpm. On the first chart, there wasn't any fuel moving through the B line until the engine was over 3500 rpm, so Jeff changed to a lighter spring in the vacuum diaphragm housing.

Test two was run only to 5500 rpm at the same acceleration rate of 200rpm per second. Again, we experienced the roar of a healthy small-block under full power. As the tach zoomed past 5000rpm the engine was really screaming. To a first-time observer it seemed that the en-

Pistons come in every style imaginable. Starting at the lower left and moving clockwise are a stock cast piston, stock forged piston, hypereutectic piston with high silicone content, flat-top forged piston, forged piston with low silicone content (race only), and two dished pistons for supercharged engines.

Chevy big-block heads like these come with canted valves, making this a semi-hemi design and providing good breathing characteristics.

By the time everything is hooked up, the engine is a maze of wires and plumbing.

Connecting rods come in various styles as well. Starting at the lower left and going clockwise you can see a stock rod with new bolts, stock rod after polishing and shot peening, street replacement rod of 4340 steel, H-D

rod machined from 4340 forged steel, ultimate full-competition rod with H-beam, and a drag-race only all-aluminum rod.

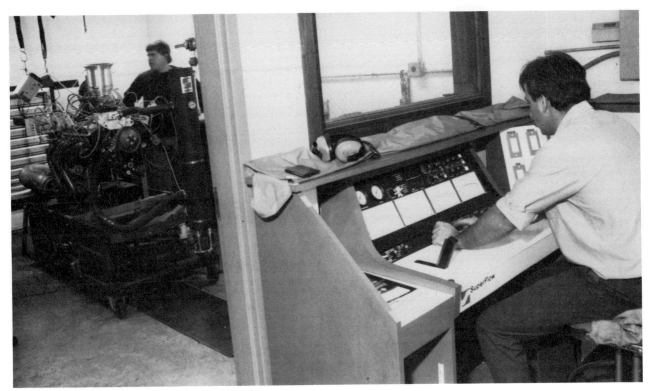

Because of the extreme noise and possibility of flying shrapnel, the dyno must be enclosed in a separate room.

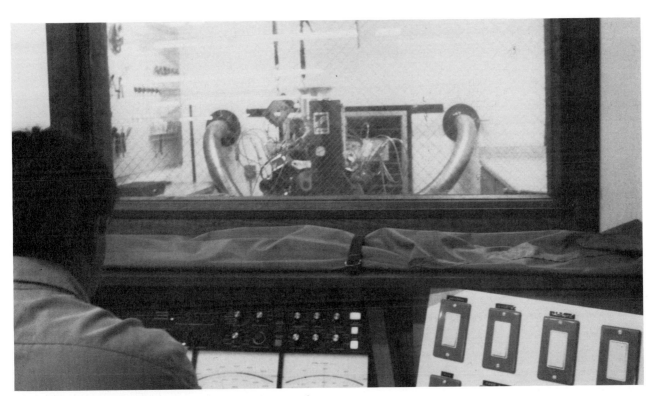

Dave runs the engine through its paces, with the rate of acceleration controlled by the dyno. Final results are contained on a printout.

An Uplifting Discussion About Camshafts

Trying to figure out which camshaft is best and why can be a confusing business. The following discussion is intended to help reduce the confusion and clarify some terms. Though your understanding may improve, you should still seek advice from the manufacturer or the shop doing the work before choosing a camshaft.

First, let's walk through two crankshaft rotations on a typical single-cylinder, four-cycle engine. Because the camshaft runs at half the speed of the crank, the camshaft will turn one complete revolution to the crankshaft's two.

Power stroke: On the beginning of the power stroke, with the piston at (or near) TDC, both valves are closed. A spark causes pressure in the cylinder to build and the piston is forced downward. As the piston nears the bottom of the cylinder, the pressure—and power production—drops off. In order to get as much of the spent gas out of the cylinder as possible, the exhaust valve opens well before the piston actually reaches bottom dead center, or BDC.

Exhaust stroke: The exhaust valve is open as this stroke begins, and it stays open during the entire 180 degrees of the exhaust stroke. In order to pack as much fresh gas as possible into the cylinder, especially during higher rpm, the intake valve actually opens before the piston hits TDC. This period during which both valves are open is known as the overlap period.

Intake stroke: As the intake stroke begins, both valves are open. By roughly twenty degrees past TDC the exhaust valve has closed, ending the overlap period. The intake valve remains open during the rest of the intake stroke.

Compression stroke: Though it would seem best to close the intake valve when the piston hits BDC, the gas and air are coming into the cylinder with a certain momentum (especially at higher rpm) and the piston doesn't start to build pressure until it is partway up into the cylinder. For these reasons, the intake valve stays open partway into the compression stroke.

Duration: Duration is the number of crankshaft degrees that the valve is open. If an intake valve started to open at thirty degrees before TDC and stayed open forty degrees past TDC, it would have a total duration of 250 degrees (30 + 180 + 40 degrees).

When comparing duration figures from one cam to another, it is important to use the correct duration specification. In order to keep everything equal, most manufacturers provide both advertised duration figures and duration figures for after the lifter has achieved 0.050in of lift. By adopting this standard, cam manufacturers make it easier to compare apples to apples.

The Iskenderian 262 Hydraulic Super cam, for example, advertises 262 degrees of duration for both intake and exhaust. The duration after the valves have achieved 0.050in of lift and before they lose the last 0.050in of lift (on the downside of the ramp) is 208 degrees. By the way, Isky claims this cam with 0.290in of lift and a lobe separation angle of 108 degrees is an excellent choice for a street rod with an automatic and a street converter.

As a rule of thumb, a cam with longer duration will have more high-rpm power than a cam with less duration. Too much duration on the street will give you a car without much power at lower rpm, where you tend to need it most.

Overlap: As already described, overlap is that period of time when both the intake and exhaust valves are open. Some cam manufacturers are starting to use a new term, lobe separation angle, instead of overlap. It is the distance in cam degrees between the centerline of the intake and exhaust lobe. Similar to overlap, the separation angle is more comprehensive. Not only does it include overlap information (a narrow angle means more overlap), it also provides more valve timing information than the simple overlap specification alone. In general, a cam with more overlap will tend to have a power band that is narrower and occurs at a higher rpm than a cam with less overlap.

Intake lobe centerline: This is a timing specification often provided on the cam card. It is the position of the piston and crank when the intake valve is at its maximum opening. If the intake lobe centerline is 110 degrees, the crankshaft will have turned 110 degrees past TDC when the intake valve has achieved maximum lift. Measured in crankshaft degrees, intake lobe centerline can be compared with the lobe separation angle to indicate the amount of advance the camshaft has relative to the crankshaft.

To fully understand how intake lobe centerline affects engine performance and timing requires a short explanation. At TDC, or zero crankshaft degrees, with the marks lined up on the timing gears the cam has both lobes pointed up. This is the middle (or roughly the middle) of the overlap period, and it also places the cam in the approximate middle of the lobe separation angle. If the same cam with 110 degrees of intake lobe centerline had a lobe separation angle of 110 degrees, it would be said to be zero degrees advanced.

In other words, starting at TDC, the crankshaft moves through 110 degrees of rotation, or 55 degrees of cam rotation, to put the intake valve at maximum lift. Because 55 is half of the lobe separation angle, the cam was in the exact middle of the overlap period (half the lobe separation angle) when the piston was at TDC.

If the same cam with a 110 degree lobe separation angle specified a 106 degree intake lobe centerline, then that cam is said to be 4 degrees advanced. The crank would turn only 106 degrees to arrive at the high point of the intake lobe, thus the cam was installed "advanced." Many cams are installed slightly advanced in order to compensate for timing chain wear which will retard the timing.

Valve lift: This is simply the amount the valve is lifted off the valve seat. More lift would seem to add more power, although there are trade-offs here just like everywhere else. For example, open the intake valve too far, too quick, and it runs into the piston. Even if it didn't run into the piston, the higher the lift (at a given duration) the faster it must move in going from the closed to the open position. Moving the valve that fast puts enormous stress on the valvetrain and requires stout springs (which create even more stress) to keep the valve following the steep ramp when the valve closes.

Designing a cam is very much a matter of matching the lobe shapes, lift, duration, and timing to a particular set of operating conditions. Timing is always critical; to produce power, air and fuel must be encouraged to enter the cylinder. Once burned, those fumes must likewise be encouraged to exit the cylinder so another fresh charge can enter. Considering only the oversimplified situation presented above, long duration would seem a good

thing. Taken to the extreme, however, valves that are open too long are seldom closed and there is no meaningful power stroke.

In particular, an exhaust valve that is open too far into the intake stroke (a lengthy overlap period or narrow lobe separation angle) might work well on a high-rpm drag race motor. At low rpm, however, the engine has low vacuum (the exhaust valve is open for so much of the intake stroke that it acts like a giant vacuum leak), runs rough, and may spit exhaust pressure into the carburetor or allow raw gas to run right out into the exhaust pipe.

The cam that's right for you will depend on a whole list of variables, including the type of transmission you choose, engine displacement, carburetor, heads, and the type of driving you do. Getting that perfect cam means asking the right questions and being honest about the type of power you want and the kind of driving you do.

The only real problem with the engine was a reluctance of the vacuum-controlled secondaries to open. Here, Jeff Fiala from Wheeler removes the diaphragm for a spring change.

The air horn has a small fan inside of it—to monitor the amount of air entering the engine. Each of the two fuel lines is monitored so the operator can tell how much fuel is running through the primary and secondary, and when the secondary kicks in.

Looking into the R&R Performance dyno room—through the reinforced glass window. As mentioned, hearing protection is needed during testing.

Ron Quarnstrom from R&R checks the porting work results with the flow bench.

gine couldn't possibly stand this kind of high-rpm running, but of course it did.

It took a little more tinkering to get the secondaries to open to Jeff's satisfaction. Everything else looked good. Air-fuel ratios were in the 12.8 to 13.2 range, the right place to be for maximum power. On run number three they ran the motor to 6250rpm. Corrected power figures (corrected for temperature and atmospheric pressure so dyno runs from different days with different conditions can be compared) showed peak figures of 386lb-ft at 4750rpm and 384hp at 5750rpm.

Jeff was pleased with the output of the little 350 built on a budget and decided to add a little timing to see if that would help the horsepower. Moving the timing two degrees gave us almost 400lb-ft of torque and 396hp. (Some of the gain

seen during the first few runs was because the engine was breaking in as the runs were performed and worked a little better with each pull.)

The next hour was spent in the quest for more horsepower. More timing, better fuel, a spacer under the carburetor—Jeff tried all the tricks in order to make the 350 run as well as it possibly could. In spite of his efforts, the little Bow-Tie engine wouldn't show us 400hp.

Before shutting down the dyno, Jeff and Dave ran the engine through a series of cruise tests. These tests are designed to simulate the rpm and load that the engine will encounter during a cruise condition. Achieving maximum horsepower is fine, but most engines spend the vast majority of their time on the highway at less than 3000rpm. Jeff and Dave ran the engine at

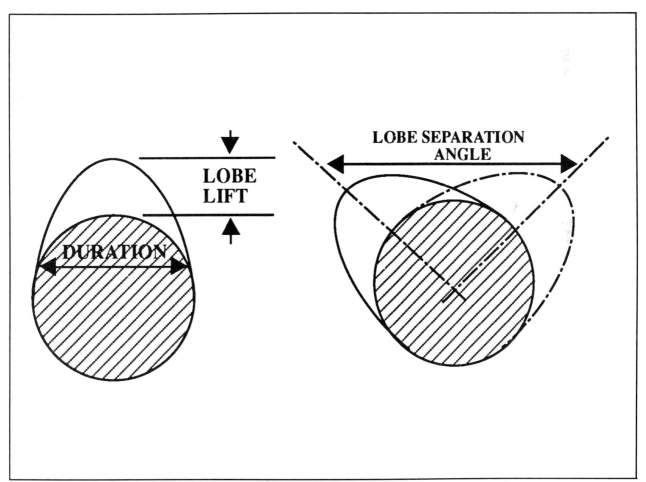

Duration is the number of degrees that the valve is open, measured in crankshaft degrees. Modern cams use a duration figure @.050in of lift so one brand of cam can be measured against another. Lobe lift is simply the amount the cam lobe lifts the lifter (not the same as the amount it lifts the valve, due to the rocker

arm ratio). The lobe separation angle is the number of cam degrees between the intake lobe and the exhaust lobe (the standard is 110 degrees). Intake lobe centerline is a timing specification that relates the point of highest intake lift to the position of the piston.

2500rpm and dialed in about as much load (usually about 30hp) as is required to propel a typical car down a level road. Gradually the load was increased in stages, keeping the rpm level. The printout showed an air-fuel ratio of 14.0:1, gradually changing to 12.8:1 as the throttle went full open. The idea here was to check the air-fuel ratio during cruise conditions and also to check and see when the power valve opened.

You need the power valve to fatten up the ratio when the engine is under full power, yet you don't want it to open too soon and waste fuel. Typical power valves (different models are available for Holley carburetors and many others) open at 6-10in of vacuum (inHg). A valve that opens at 6in will open later than one that opens at 10inHg. The 350 opened at just over 6in of vacuum, a good reading for most cars.

Following the cruise test, the engine was pulled off the dyno for the trip back to the Wheeler shop. If all this seems like a lot of work, consider what we learned: The motor didn't leak, it ran well, and it had the right air-fuel ratios throughout the rpm range to achieve both good power under full load and good economy under part-throttle operation. That's a whole lot more than most builders know when they slide that new engine between the rails of their new hot rod.

Rodders often complain that the small-block Ford is too long to install in a street rod. Art has a solution: a billet water pump of his own design and manufacture, a pump that makes a Ford the same length (or just a little shorter than) as a Chevy.

Chapter 3

Injection Inspection

More and more street rods and hot rods are turning up with fuel injection under the hood. Besides that certain sex appeal offered by a polished tuned port injection (TPI) unit, there are some definite benefits to fuel injection in terms of power, driveability, and a clean tailpipe.

In order to help you understand these systems and decide which might be best for your situation, this chapter offers a short history, a look at current port fuel injection systems offered by the factories, and an overview of some high-performance fuel injection systems. After reading this chapter, the street rodder who wants to run fuel injection should be qualified to buy a good system that meets the needs of the new car he or she is trying to build.

And if you think it's blasphemy to run anything but a Holley on a street rod engine, well, read on anyway. You'll have a better understanding of how the injection works on your daily driver.

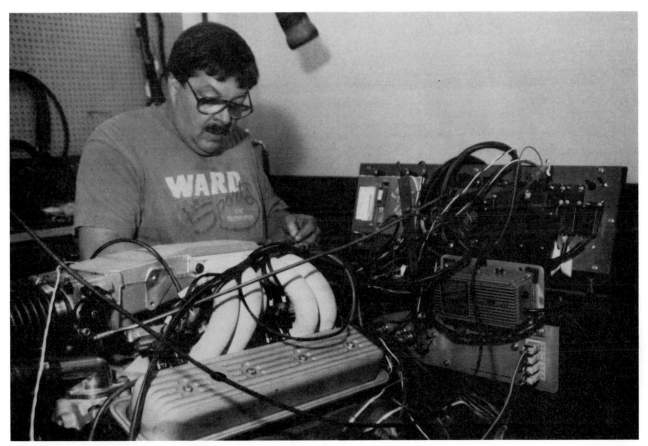

Myron Cottrell, the man behind TPIS, hooks up another fuel injection system on a dyno engine during some of his extensive testing.

This airfoil, developed after lengthy testing on the TPIS flow bench and dyno, adds significantly to the maximum flow of a stock TPI. In addition to adding to the total cubic feet per minute, this little foil helps to reduce turbulence in the plenum at moderate airflow.

A stock GM throttle body, with the TPIS airfoil installed.

Fuel Injection—Some Early History

We may think of fuel injection as something new and high-tech. Yet, the idea of fuel injection is as old as the internal combustion engine. In fact, when Otto Diesel had trouble making his early engine designs run, he tried *injecting* the fuel—coal dust, in this case.

Early carburetors were crude devices at best. The first fuel injection systems were built simply to eliminate the carburetor. In the air, early pilots discovered firsthand the shortcomings of carburetion—where a little carburetor icing or a fire meant more than a long walk home.

Wilbur and Orville Wright built their own fuel injection systems for their flights at Kitty Hawk, North Carolina, and other airplane designers soon followed suit.

In 1912 a bright young German engineer by the name of Robert Bosch converted a two-stroke outboard motor to fuel injection. The results were encouraging and developmental work was well under way when the war came between Bosch and his work.

Most of these early fuel injection designs were direct injection systems with mechanical controls. Direct injection uses a very high pressure pump (over 1,000 pounds per square inch, or psi) to inject fuel directly into the cylinder. Many of these designs were converted diesel injection systems.

World War II accelerated the development of fuel injection both here and in Europe. The Robert Bosch Corporation, as it was eventually called, and the maker of the Mercedes automobile applied direct injection to some aviation engines, obtaining more than 1200hp from a 33 liter V-12. General Motors was engaged in similar work during the war, assisting Allison Aircraft with fuel injection designs.

One of the first postwar fuel injection applications came in 1949 when the first fuel-injected Offenhauser appeared at Indianapolis. The system was designed by Stuart Hilborn and Bill Travers. By 1953, it was standard equipment on Offy-powered cars.

The system came to be known as Hilborn fuel injection and soon crossed over into other types

This Mini-Ram manifold from TPIS is a one-piece casting. The low-profile design means lots of hood clearance and a boost of over 100hp compared to stock.

of racing. The Hilborn system differed from others, however; it was *indirect* (or port type) injection, with fuel injected into the intake port just ahead of the intake valve. The port injection design meant fuel could be sprayed at a much lower pressure, eliminating the expensive and noisy high-pressure fuel pump.

At about the same time, GM began researching practical applications of this new fuel injection technology. Zora Arkus-Duntov, the genius behind the Corvette, wanted fuel injection for street use and began working with John Dolza, a GM engineer who had experience working with Allison Aircraft during WW II.

Zora and John chose a port injection system with mostly mechanical controls. The key to any good fuel injection system is the precise measurement of the air mass entering the engine so the correct amount of fuel can be injected. The system built by the Rochester Products Division measures the air mass as it first enters the engine.

The new Rochester fuel injection system was introduced on the 1957 Corvette. Pontiac, in an attempt to keep up with the corporate Joneses,

offered the same system on some Bonnevilles. More than 2,000 fuel-injected Corvettes were sold during 1957. Unfortunately, the Rochester system worked better in the lab than it did in practice. Chevrolet offered the Rochester system until 1965, but only in very limited numbers.

As GM was eliminating fuel injection from the options list, another manufacturer in another part of the world was moving in exactly the opposite direction.

Evolution of Modern Fuel Injection Systems

During the mid-1960s, German-based auto maker Volkswagen asked the Robert Bosch company to design a fuel injection system capable of meeting future US emissions standards. The system Bosch developed for Volkswagen became known as D-Jetronic.

D-Jetronic was a port or indirect fuel injection system. The difference in this new system was the completely electronic control. Fuel was injected by solenoid type injectors mounted just upstream of the intake valves. The length of each injection pulse was determined by an early electronic control module, or ECM (known today as the computer).

These siamesed runners are from TPIS, though similar designs are available from other manufacturers (in- *cluding Chevrolet). The runners pass significantly more air than their stock counterparts.*

The stock tuned port injection can be quite restrictive at higher rpm. To answer the need for more airflow, TPIS has developed the Big Mouth manifold.

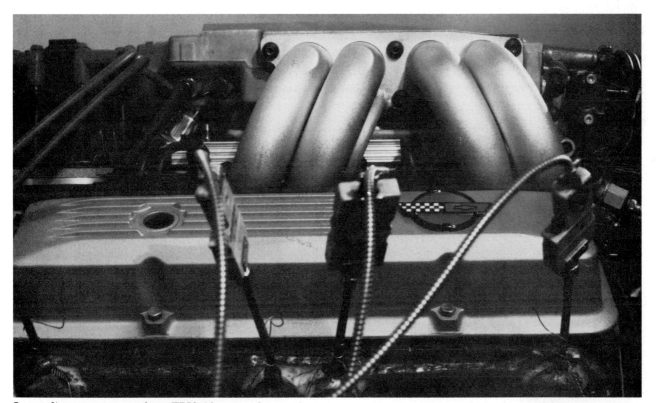

Large diameter runners from TPIS (they are also available from other companies). These runners are hard to tell from stock, yet they flow significantly more air.

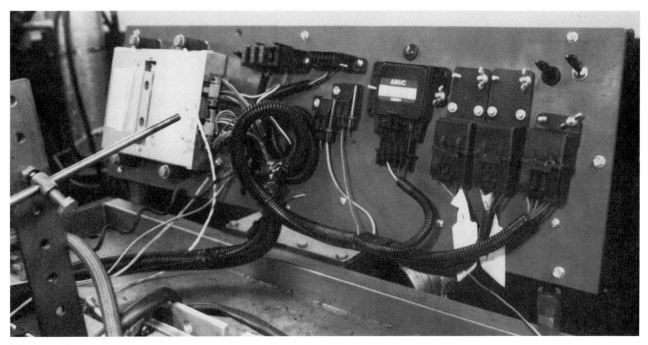

The control board on the TPIS dyno. On the right is a group of three relays—the three necessary for a GM mass air system; next is the single relay necessary for a speed-density system; and on the far left is the computer with its PROM.

The four basic GM computers: #7730, for MAP sensed (speed-density) Corvettes, Firebirds, and Camaros from 1990-1992; #7165, used with mass air systems from 1986-1989; #6870, used with Corvettes in 1985; and #9278, used with the new LT-1 engines (another speed-density system).

Rather than try to sample the amount of air mass directly, Bosch used rpm and vacuum sensors (for engine speed and load) to give an approximation of total mass air. The control module used this indirect mass air measurement, modified by inputs from temperature and throttle position sensors, to determine the timing and duration of each injection pulse. More sophisticated examples of this same basic system are still used on many GM vehicles today—known as speed-density systems.

As promised, the new Bosch system provided good power and met emission standards that weren't even in place yet. Why, you might ask, was this collection of voodoo from Germany able to reduce so dramatically the amount of carbon monoxide, hydrocarbons, and assorted crud emitted from the tailpipe? Let's take a look.

Fuel Injection Theory

The goal of any fuel delivery system is to deliver the correct amounts of fuel and air to the cylinder in a combustible condition. Physics tells us that a ratio of 14.7 parts air to 1 part gas is an ideal, or "stoichiometric" ratio. On paper, that says there will be a perfect burn. The fuel delivery engineer, however, is faced with a series of problems outside such a formula.

First, the ideal ratio isn't always the same. Cold engines need a richer mixture, and accelerating engines need a little extra fuel for maximum power. Second, for complete combustion the gasoline must atomize and mix thoroughly with the air. Third, the correct ratio must be delivered under a variety of conditions, including temperature extremes and cornering forces.

Before examining fuel injection, it might help to look at the alternative—carburetors. At the heart of most carburetors is a venturi. A venturi is simply a restriction in a pipe. According to the laws of physics, as the air speeds up to pass through the venturi, the pressure drops. Gasoline, under atmospheric pressure in the float bowl, is pushed through the jet and into the opening in the venturi, where it mixes with the air.

Presuming we have the correct mix of air and gas, the mixture must still travel through the in-

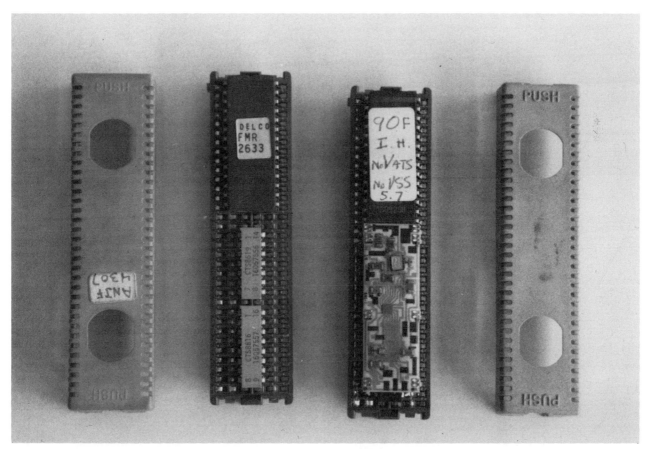

On the left is the typical PROM used with a GM mass air system (with its plastic cover), and on the right is a PROM used with a speed-density system. These

PROMs contain the information specific to each model or custom application.

take manifold to each cylinder. The path from carburetor to cylinder is seldom straight and narrow, and the relative weight of gasoline becomes a problem as the mixture makes those tight turns. The gas sometimes separates from the air stream and puddles in the manifold runners.

The net result of all this is a system that fails on occasion to provide an ideal air-fuel mixture and has further trouble delivering that ideal mixture to each cylinder.

Fuel injection offers a number of advantages when compared to carburetion. Some of these advantages are inherent in the design, while others are the result of modern-day computer technology.

At the heart of the fuel injection system are the injectors themselves. Gasoline must be mixed with air before it will burn. The mist created by the injection nozzles breaks the gasoline into very small particles, and smaller particles mix more readily with the air. Equally important, a very small particle is more likely to obtain enough oxygen for complete combustion, and complete combustion means more power and fewer waste products at the tailpipe.

Because this fuel mist is delivered just upstream from the intake valve, there is no problem of fuel and air separation in the intake manifold or different amounts of fuel being delivered to different cylinders.

Modern port injection systems tie all the injectors into a common fuel ring. Using a solenoid for an injector and controlling the solenoid with an ECM means great precision in delivering the correct amount of fuel. Modern systems do a good job of measuring the air mass (more on that later). That air mass measurement, coupled with information from temperature, rpm, and throttle position sensors, enables the ECM to deliver an exact mixture for a given set of engine conditions. This precision is simply more than most carburetors can match.

The precision is enhanced even more through the use of an oxygen sensor. The sensor samples the oxygen content in the exhaust. If the mixture becomes too rich or too lean, the sensor signals the ECM so the mixture can be corrected. (When input from the oxygen sensor is being used by the ECM, the entire system is said to be operat-

This is a remanufactured #7165 computer from GM with the correct PROM and plastic cover.

ing in a "closed loop." "Open loop" operation will be discussed later.)

Today's Fuel Injection

The Bosch systems that showed up on those early Volkswagens and other imports were considered "pretty weird" by most mechanics of the day. In fact, those systems were the forerunners to many of today's fuel injection systems. The early Jetronic systems were among the first to combine the inherent advantages of port type fuel injection with the precision and durability of electronic control.

The next generation of electronic fuel injection systems from Bosch offered two major improvements. First, the air mass was measured directly with an air flap mounted in the intake air stream. Second, advances in integrated circuit technology made it possible to simplify and improve the control module. These changes made

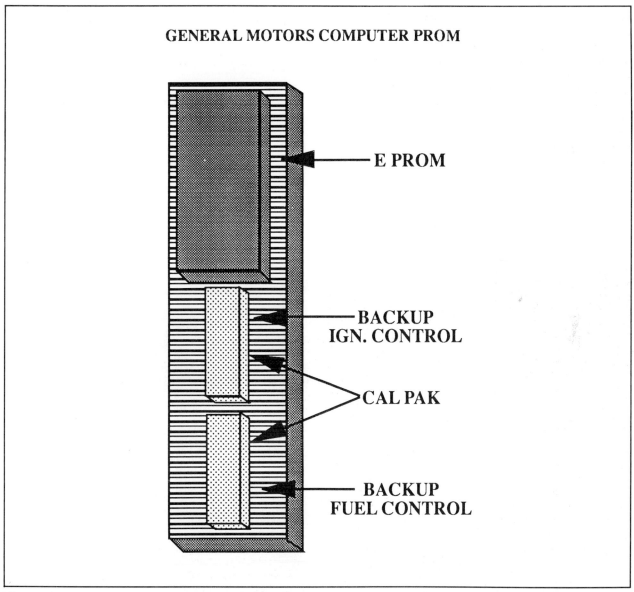

GENERAL MOTORS COMPUTER PROM

E PROM

BACKUP IGN. CONTROL

CAL PAK

BACKUP FUEL CONTROL

This is the "chip" or PROM that plugs into a GM TPI computer. Though the entire thing is known as the PROM, it contains the E PROM, which is where the instructions are stored for your particular car, and the Calibration Package. The Cal Pak contains the instructions for "limp-home" mode—the mode the computer changes to when it senses some kind of problem with the system. In limp-home mode the fuel and ignition curves are very limited—that's why you don't want to buy an aftermarket harness that runs the system on limp-home mode all the time. The PROM for a speed/density system looks slightly different and contains very different instructions.

Installing fuel injection on your non-fuel-injected car requires an aftermarket harness like this one from TPIS. Be sure to buy a harness that has the capacity to run the system in the closed loop mode.

the system both more accurate and more dependable.

This second-generation system from Bosch set the pattern that would be followed by both Ford and GM in designing fuel injection systems for their high-performance small-block V-8s. Both companies use port injection with electronic control. Some of these systems measure the mass of air directly while others do it indirectly, but both offer performance, economy, and emissions that were only an engineer's dream just a few years ago.

Most readers are interested in fuel injection mainly as an aftermarket addition to their street rod. But before trying to determine which system is best for your application, it might help to examine the new systems in greater detail.

Because most of the engines—and thus most of the fuel injection systems—being bolted in to street rods and hot rods are from GM, we'll use that system as an example. Unless otherwise noted, the following comments on factory systems refer to the GM tuned port system as seen on late-model Corvettes, Camaros, and Firebirds.

High-Performance Factory Fuel Injection

The current fuel injection systems used by both Ford and GM in their high-performance V-

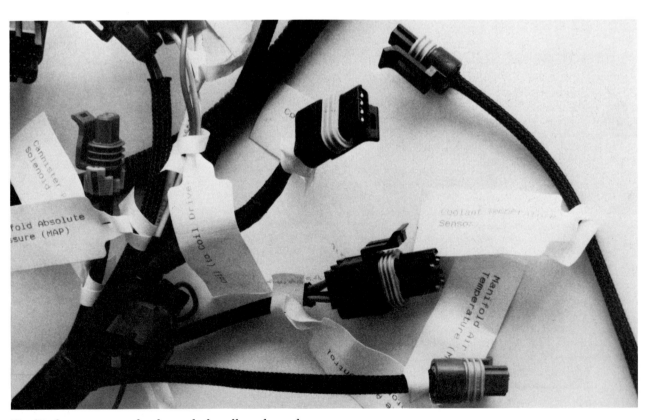

Quality harnesses are clearly marked, well made, and use weatherproof connections.

8s are port type injection with electronic control. There is one fuel injector for each cylinder, mounted in the intake manifold just ahead of the intake valve.

As with earlier systems, each injector is actually a solenoid. GM injectors fire once per crankshaft revolution. The ECM determines the pulse width—that is, how long the injector will stay open. TPI systems from GM can be broken down according to how they measure the air mass entering the engine. Some of the earlier systems, from 1985 to 1989, used a direct measure of the air mass and are known as mass air systems. Starting in 1990, GM switched to a speed-density system that relies on indirect measurement of the air mass entering the engine. A switch back to the mass air type of system in 1993 has been predicted.

People often ask, which system is the best? There is no best one; like anything else each system has advantages and disadvantages, especially when viewed from the unique perspective of a street rodder.

The speed-density system uses a sophisticated electronic vacuum gauge known as a manifold absolute pressure sensor (or MAP) to measure the load on the engine. This MAP sensor, in combination with rpm information and inputs from temperature and throttle position sensors, provides the basic information the ECM needs to determine pulse width and timing.

With a mass air system, the amount of air entering the engine is measured directly. The mass airflow sensor (MAF), sometimes known as a hot wire, measures the resistance of a piece of platinum wire in the intake tract. The wire is heated by current from the ECM; air moving past the wire tends to cool it, changing the resistance of the wire. This change in resistance is interpreted by the ECM as a change in airflow. In addition to the signal from the mass air sensor, these systems use inputs from throttle position, air temperature, and rpm before determining the amount and timing of the injection pulse.

These modern TPI systems have evolved a great deal from the Bosch systems that preceded them. The ECM in either type of system is able

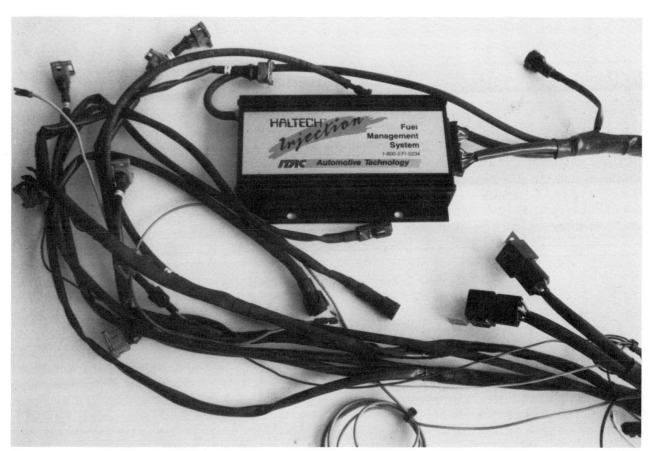

If you install fuel injection or want to upgrade from factory fuel injection, a number of aftermarket systems are available. This Haltech computer can be pro- *grammed by the owner. Not all programmable systems offer the same degree of control, however.*

Roddy Mears from EFI Technology works with Myron Cottrell on a test of their new system. The EFI computer or ECU (electronic control unit) can be pro- *grammed—both ignition and fuel curves—using a laptop computer.*

to fine-tune the amount of fuel being injected by analyzing its own exhaust sample. The oxygen sensor mounted in the exhaust system signals the ECM of any need for more or less fuel. This feedback or self-regulating mode used during idle and cruise situations is known as closed loop. Open loop describes those conditions, like wide-open throttle, when the ECM operates without the input of the oxygen sensor.

Tuned port injection has a few more tricks up its fuel-injected sleeve, like idle speed control through an idle air control, and ignition timing control. Because the ECM knows engine speed and load (as well as air and engine temperature, and throttle position), it is in a very good position to determine the appropriate ignition timing. Through the use of a knock sensor the ECM is able to pick an ideal ignition timing figure and then roll it back slightly if that optimum figure results in a knock (another nice self-regulating feature).

Realistically, the major difference between the two types of TPI systems is that the speed-density TPI is designed and programmed to work with a specific engine. These systems only know how much fuel to add during a given situation because they've been "mapped." The map provided by the factory dictates that a given set of conditions creates a particular pulse width. If you change the camshaft or add a set of headers the amount of air moving through that engine changes—but the map remains the same. Yes, you can change the map (contained on the PROM, which we will discuss shortly), but it can be tough to get just the right map for your particular set of modifications.

A mass air type of tuned port injection is better suited to people who want to modify their engines because any increase in airflow will automatically create additional fuel. There is no need to give the computer a new set of instructions.

At this point it might be instructive to describe the ECM—the computer, or black box—that drives these modern TPI systems.

The computer truly is a black box, in the sense that it is sealed from any tinkering on our part. The only part you can readily change is the PROM (programmable read only memory) chip.

Myron and Roddy hook up the EFI system on the dyno motor. This system (or software) can be hooked up with *stock GM TPI hardware or aftermarket manifold and runners.*

The PROM contains the specific timing and fuel injection instructions for each specific model of car. By installing an aftermarket PROM (sometimes known as a chip) you are able to change the amount and timing of the injection pulse under certain conditions as well as the ignition timing and curve.

Another component in the computer is the Cal Pak or calibration package. The Cal Pak contains the instruction for the "limp home" mode. Limp home is one of the computer's three basic operating modes (the other two being open loop and closed loop). The computer operates in the limp home mode whenever it senses a major malfunction. In this mode, the computer uses a very limited fuel curve and limits ignition timing to a total of twenty-two degrees.

How to Install TPI on Your Street Rod

Being basically a dissatisfied group of malcontents, street rodders and hot rodders have been tinkering with factory fuel injection from the very start. The factory wiring harness is anything but simple, containing hundreds of wires and more than a few resistors and relays. Not all

A look inside the EFI computer. There is no slot for a PROM because you can "burn your own PROM" when you plug in your computer to change the fuel delivery or the ignition timing.

of those wires are needed on all cars however, and simplified wiring harnesses have been available for street rods and other aftermarket users for some time now.

Installing fuel injection on your street rod can be a relatively simple matter of buying a complete TPI engine at the junkyard and matching that engine with an electric fuel pump and aftermarket wiring harness. If horsepower is the name of your game, then large-tube runners, big-mouth manifolds, and large throttle bodies are available. For the serious technoid and horsepower freak, components designed to pass more air can be connected to a unique ECM—one that you can program yourself.

In discussing the various fuel injection alternatives that are available as a retrofit, it might be easiest to start with the simplest and move on to the more complex (and costly) systems.

The easiest way to install a GM tuned port system on your street rod is to bring home a complete TPI 305 or 350 from a late-model wreck. Once you have installed the engine, install an electric fuel pump and buy a wiring harness from a reputable firm.

Most of the harnesses contain plug-ins for the injectors and the various TPI components and three additional wires: one that supplies power to the electric fuel pump, one that connects to battery power, and one that connects to a source that's hot when the ignition switch is turned on. You need an electric speedometer or a PROM that compensates for the lack of the speedometer input. And you also need a second, return line to the gas tank.

The fuel pump can be installed in the tank by adapting part of the factory tank to your street rod gas tank, or by mounting an electric pump of the right capacity in the line close to the fuel tank. The in-tank location is ideal, as it keeps the pump quiet and cool—though plenty of fuel-injected factory cars (many European makes) mount their electric pumps outside the tank.

Not all aftermarket wiring harnesses are created equal. Be sure the one you buy uses the full capacity of the ECM. Some early harnesses

Not all GM HEI distributors are the same. If you are installing a TPI system, be sure to get the right distributor (with threaded holddown screws as seen on the right) and be sure the plug-ins match up with the rest of the wiring harness.

didn't use the PROM at all and ran the system in limp home mode (during limp home the system runs off the Cal Pak and uses a very limited set of instructions to operate the engine). Running a TPI in limp home mode is kind of like using a supercomputer to play Nintendo—you just aren't using the full capacity of the system. Be sure your harness will allow the system to run in all three modes (that way you can put an oxygen sensor in the exhaust so it will run in the closed loop mode), and be sure it is designed for your system (either speed-density or mass air).

If the system is a speed-density setup, you need to either leave the engine stock with the equipment it carried from the factory, or find an aftermarket PROM manufacturer that can help you get the right PROM for your unique set of modifications.

The HEI ignition that came (you hope) with the engine you installed is hard to beat. Unless you're going racing, be sure to get the distributor with the engine so you can just plug it in when you hook up the harness. If you want a little

more ignition timing or a faster ignition curve, it can be done by changing the PROM.

Sometimes, injectors that have been in the junkyard for a few years don't want to fire. Such a problem will show up as a dead cylinder and can be traced to that one bad injector. Dealerships and shops that do a lot of fuel injection work have equipment to clean injectors. There are also cleaners that you can add to the gas or bolt on to the fuel rail. If you want precision, then you can have the injectors blueprinted by a company like TPIS in Chaska, Minnesota. TPIS will clean and check your injectors, or you can exchange them for a set of matched injectors that shoot a specified amount of gas at a given pressure.

Speaking of injectors, the various catalogs list them either by the type of engine they are designed to run with or by the amount of fuel they put out per hour of use. The trouble with the latter type is that the pressures aren't always the same, so you can't compare apples to apples. Most V-8 injectors put out plenty of fuel, even for modified engines. Myron Cottrell, owner of TPIS,

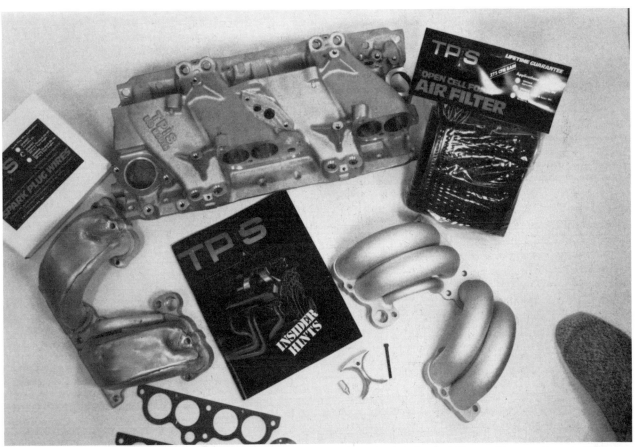

You can increase the airflow of your stock TPI system one step at a time or all at once. Displayed is a sampling of the equipment available from TPIS, everything *from a simple airfoil to a big-mouth manifold and siamesed runners.*

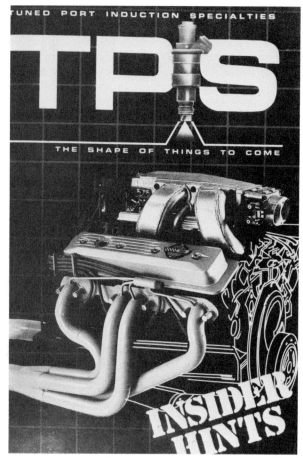

TUNED PORT INDUCTION SPECIALTIES

TPIS

THE SHAPE OF THINGS TO COME

INSIDER HINTS

There aren't many books that address the needs of aftermarket fuel injection installation and modification. Myron's Insider Hints *contains many charts and graphs, as well as some very useful information for rodders running TPI on their car.*

has run 305 injectors in larger engines without any trouble. The best advice is to consult someone who understands fuel injection before assuming you need higher capacity injectors for your hot rod.

Hot Rod Tuned Port Injection

The tuned port injection system manufactured by General Motors is one of the best fuel injection systems offered on any car in the world, though it has shortcomings along with its strong points. Designed for torque and built around the 305 engine, TPI is a torque monster at low rpm, but it peaks early and doesn't provide enough air for high-rpm use (over 5000rpm). In a recent dyno test done at the TPIS facility, a 383ci small-block equipped with stock TPI hardware and a near-stock PROM pulled more than 360lb-ft at 2500rpm while a 750 Holley on the same engine pulled only 284lb-ft. Of course, at 6000rpm the numbers were reversed as the Holley-equipped

Technology Whose Time Has Come

Myron Cottrell, owner of TPIS in Chaska, Minnesota, is a man who enjoys what he does. And what he does best is explore the possibilities of fuel injection as applied to high-performance automobiles. In addition to his own research and development, Myron has done research work for foreign automobile firms and various race teams. His personal projects include a small-block-equipped Firebird that he races at the Sports Car Club of America (SCCA) track in Brainerd, Minnesota, and a very fast 1985 Corvette. The few hours spent with Myron were very enjoyable—especially after the interview when Myron handed me the keys to his Corvette.

Q: *Myron, why don't you start with a little background about yourself.*

Myron: In 1972, I was working as a truck mechanic at a Ford dealership and building motors in my garage at home. I got an opportunity to interview for a job with the Minnesota state vocational system that was starting up at the time. I ended up with the task of writing the curriculum for automotive machinist. It turned out to be a ten-year job with good benefits, and I learned a great deal when I was there. I had a lot of fun, we did a lot of dyno work, had a good rapport with the students. It was a real good experience for me. During that whole time I continued to build high-performance engines at home.

About ten years ago I left the vo-tech school and we put up our building here. After we put up the building I was able to do work on a larger scope and build a more professional image. At about that time the first tuned port fuel injection system came out. In 1986 I bought a system from the junkyard for a thousand bucks—a lot of money at that time.

I took the wiring harness apart and figured out how to make it work and what the fuel curve and ignition curves looked like. We started with the hot rod approach—'what could I do to make this system make more power?' The first thing I did was adjust fuel pressure. We cut open that lid and put a bolt and a nut in there to adjust the pressure. My computer background isn't real good, but I do have a lot of street savvy...and so I started working with pressures and then I worked on the airflow.

We designed that little air foil that bolts into the center of the stock throttle bodies. We made the first ones from clay and then made prototypes out of balsa wood.

We discovered that they not only make more full-throttle power, but that they seem to get rid of some midrange fluttering probably caused by some turbulence in the airflow at part throttle. So I went way out on the limb and had the patterns made and had 2,000 manufactured. We sent one to *Hot Rod* magazine and they ran a new product release and the product really took off.

About that time I ran into a fella who does great programming and now he works exclusively for us developing new PROMs for the TPI systems.

We have collected products, like the large-tube runners from Arizona Speed and Marine, and we've made our own products, like the Big Mouth manifold and the Mini Ram. We manufacture our own header and rear exhaust for the Corvette. We put together our Fast Pak that includes the air foil and the regulator and our own spiral-wound plug wires.

Q: *Why are you such a great believer in fuel injection?*

Myron: On the surface, from a horsepower standpoint, carburetion and fuel injection can be very close. Especially when you're dealing with a Holley and a good intake versus an OEM fuel injection system—if horsepower is your only goal the Holley will win. But there's so much more to engine design and performance, especially on the street. You have to drive it, you need the broadest possible power range, you need to turn the engine slowly for good mileage, and you need to be emissions responsible. Modern fuel injection does everything that a carburetor does and so much more.

Fuel injection is very, very exciting today because there is so much you can do. We have systems that can adjust each individual cylinder's fuel and ignition. You can take a Corvette like mine, with 490hp, a car that goes 202mph, gets 24.5mpg, and goes through the emission station [in Minnesota, this is an idle sniff test]. It will pull from 500 to over 7000rpm without missing a beat. We're seeing Corvette motors with 100,000 miles on them with almost no cylinder wear. The rod bearings look like new and the ring lands are not all beat out—thanks to computer controls. The precise air-fuel ratio and knock sensor mean that the driver can pump the pedal until he or she's got a sore knee and not wash down the cylinder walls.

Another thing that fuel injection does, because you're injecting fuel and not drawing it through, is to allow you to do some different things with runners and volumes which you can't do with a carburetor. With a carburetor you need to generate velocity to keep the fuel in suspension, atomized. So now you have the option of a bigger throttle body. You can use 1,000cfm throttle bodies on street cars, where you wouldn't consider going much over 600cfm with a carbureted street engine. You aren't drawing the fuel out of an orifice, you are injecting it under pressure.

You can also run big camshafts with lots of overlap and not have the problem of running a lot of unburned exhaust out the tailpipe at low rpm. And you don't need a certain vacuum level to run the ignition advance.

There's a new system from EFI Technology that will do everything that the systems run on an Indy car will do. It will allow the person at home to program his or her own ignition and fuel curves. And like the home computers, the price of this system is on its way down.

Q: *Going back to velocity in the intake tract, what happens if the carb gets too big, and why isn't that a problem with fuel injection?*

Myron: When the carburetor's too big for the engine, it gets lazy. I say they don't properly excite the circuitry. An analogy might be, two 4in fans in a 4in tube. If you drive one fan it will definitely move the blades of the other. If you did the same thing with the same fans in an 8in tube, the effect on the second fan is minimized. For simplicity's sake, assume that the second fan is a liquid you're trying to pull through an orifice. The term carbureted means to emulsify the fuel and present it in combustible form to the cylinder.

One thing I've always done, and it's no secret, is to use those little brass shooters in the venturi of a Holley that stick out into the air stream. You'll see six to eight more horsepower with that simple addition, and it's only a quarter-inch difference. When you understand that such small differences can make 8hp, you start to understand how delicate this whole procedure of atomizing the fuel in the right proportions and presenting it for combustion really is.

Fuel injection allows you to inject exactly the right amount of fuel, regardless of how fast the air stream is moving through the runners. That airflow no longer needs to pick up and carry the fuel, so now you are free to enlarge the size of the runners, to change their shapes—all things that you could never do with a carbureted engine.

Q: *In terms of retrofitting a junkyard engine with TPI and putting it into a street rod, what are the problems? Where do people get in trouble, and what is the best approach to take?*

Myron: The biggest problem we had at the very beginning was that people were running them in the limp home mode. Some of those first aftermarket harnesses weren't very well designed and didn't really utilize the full abilities of the system. People were jerry-rigging them and doing their own wiring harness or buying cheap harnesses. The hot rodder has learned, though, we don't get the same driveability questions we used to get. Also, there are people selling good harnesses.

In terms of doing the actual installation, it's important that the fuel pressure be right, usually 45lb. The electrical grounds must be done correctly and all the connections must be soldered. You need a good battery and charging circuit. You must run that alternator fast enough to provide 12 1/2 or 13 volts, even at idle. You have to remember that these systems consume a great deal of electricity.

There's a lot of confusion about injectors, but if they've got a 350 or 383 with a mild cam and a set of 305 injectors, we can help you make those injectors work without spending the bucks for a brand-new set of injectors.

Q: *Besides the motor and TPI hardware, what other types of equipment do you have to add for a retrofit in a street rod?*

Myron: You need an electric fuel pump and a return line. I think the hot rodders should put the pump in the tank like most of the Detroit manufacturers do—it will be much quieter. Just cut out the top of the tank in the donor car and then solder that into your gas tank on the street rod.

If you're the kind of guy who likes to tinker, add headers one day, new manifold the next, then you should get a mass air system. Some people say these mass air systems won't make horsepower. Is 542 emission legal horses from a small-block Chevy enough? That MAF [mass airflow] sensor, as we modify it, will flow 900cfm. I have not found the factory MAF sensor modified as we do it, to be a restriction up to 530hp.

The main problem with the MAF is that it's not attractive. It can be located away from the front of the motor and hidden. We provide enough wire in our harness for this.

Q: *There are some complete stand-alone fuel injection systems. Should a person install one of these, or should the street rodder start with a TPI system from GM—assuming he or she isn't interested in maximum horsepower?*

Myron: They should stick with the GM system, preferably the 1985 to 1989 mass air system. These are nonprogrammable, stick it in and run, no-brainer systems. They are easy to hook up and can be modified easily. If the street rodder is going to build a nice little car, mild motor, maybe a stock motor, and appearance is important, then maybe they want a speed-density system because they can hang an air cleaner right on the front of it and you don't have to worry about where to put the mass air sensor. But anyone who thinks that they can feed that motor through the tiny little rectangular filter that everyone runs is crazy. Look at the filter on a 750 Holley, figure out the square inches, and then look at that tiny little filter on the front of all those street rods. You probably need a minimum of 7 x 15in in area. The little ones don't pass enough air and the calibration will never be right.

Q: *Do you need an electronic speedometer?*

Myron: No, we furnish a PROM that will mask the vehicle speed sensor. Without this, it won't come back down to an idle because the computer doesn't know you stopped the car.

Q: *How can the buyer be sure of getting a good system from the junkyard or wherever, and how does he or she get a good wiring harness?*

Myron: I think you should decide on the hardware you want and then go out and be sure you get the whole system. With a mass air system you need the distributor, the mass air sensor, the ECM, the electronic spark control, three relays—MAF power, MAF burnoff, and fuel pump. You need the fuel rail and injectors all present and accounted for. You have to be careful if the system has been sitting for too long because sometimes the injectors stick and they can't always be used again.

The speed-density system is a little simpler. You need an ECM, complete intake system with MAP sensor mounted on the plenum, and the fuel

pump relay. The spark control is in the PROM, and of course you need the distributor. One clue that you have the correct distributor is that the cap has "screw-in" holddowns rather than twist-in types, and be sure too that the distributor connectors match the harness.

In terms of the harness, a good one will run in closed loop mode and it comes from a well-known manufacturer. These people installing engines should use an oxygen sensor in the exhaust (closed loop). That way, they get the full benefit of the system as it was designed.

Q: *What about someone who brings home a late-model Mustang 302 motor? Should they convert it to the GM system, or run the Ford ECM and fuel injection equipment?*

Myron: They can do either; most of the Ford stuff is speed-density, though there is a kit to convert them to the late-model Ford style mass air. It depends on the situation. I am more familiar with the GM system and there are more aftermarket PROMs available for the GM system.

Q: *If you were going to spend a little more money and you wanted a fuel-injected small-block but with more power than the stock system, what combination of equipment would you run?*

Myron: I'd run the GM ECM mass air type, and match it to our Mini Ram manifold. We have a variety of PROMs available for a setup like that. Which one I used would depend on what type of cam and how many cubes the motor was.

Q: *What about the ultimate hot rod motor? For serious horsepower, what would you build?*

Myron: If I were going to build "jewelry" I would start by deciding how many cubes I wanted. Maybe a 383 or 406 based on a 400 block—a 400 with the siamesed bores. I don't find they run any hotter than the others. I would use a 6in Crower rod and a 2in crank pin, a Callies crank, and the new Ross piston. You need a good cylinder head and cam combination. We have developed our own camshafts and they work really well with the way we port our heads. The engines respond well, they accelerate fiercely; the throttle response with our little short manifold is fantastic.

Q: *If you could sum up everything you know about fuel injection in one statement, what would you say?*

Myron: Fuel injection's time has come and it's a lot of fun for a lot of people. It does a great job of precisely controlling how much fuel is delivered, it breaks that fuel up into smaller and smaller particles so it burns well, and it does this consistently. Fuel injection allows us to have almost as much power as we want, still gives good economy, and keeps the engine's emission legal. What could be better?

Another engine ready to test on the TPIS dyno. You can tell this is a mass air system by the presence of the MAF (mass airflow) sensor mounted in the air stream just behind the air horn.

Myron Cottrell, owner and president of TPIS, uses this Firebird and a 1985 Corvette for testing his new products.

Larger diameter runners like these from Arizona Speed and Marine are available to increase the breathing ability of your TPI-equipped small-block. These can also be ordered with provisions for a nitrous setup. Arizona Speed & Marine

Larger diameter throttle bodies are available from a number of suppliers. This 1000cfm body is from Arizona Speed & Marine. Arizona Speed & Marine

engine took off and the TPI engine gasped for more air.

If you're going to run a TPI system on your car, you have to decide if great torque and reasonable horsepower up to 4500 or 5000rpm is enough. If it isn't, then you need to consider upgrades to the GM tuned port system.

In essence, any fuel injection system is a collection of hardware—the plenum, runners, manifold injectors, and all the rest—controlled by a computer or software. So when you decide to add better or more powerful fuel injection to your car, you can choose new hardware, new software, or both.

Fuel Injection Hardware

Because the stock TPI system was designed for torque and built around a relatively small engine, the system runs out of breath at about 4500rpm. Your options for getting more air to the engine start with small modifications that don't cost much, and move rapidly to the use of new components like large-tube or siamesed runners, ported manifolds, and larger throttle bodies.

Some of the simpler modifications include removing the screens from the MAF (assuming you have a mass air type of system). As delivered by the factory, this sensor has filter screens that can be rather easily removed for an additional 78cfm

Even your big-block can be equipped with TPI these days. This system and special polished brackets and *accessories are from Street & Performance.* Street & Performance

71

(for more information on these modifications, consult the TPIS book, *Insider Hints*). There are a number of other small modifications you can make to increase airflow, like the addition of an aftermarket air foil in the throttle body. If you want even more air, larger runners, ported plenums, and aftermarket intake manifolds available.

For serious horsepower freaks there are complete stand-alone systems from firms like Stealth, Accel, and TPIS. Most of these will pass 1000cfm and more. Differences include the style of plenum and the length of the runners. Before buying one of these hardware options, be sure to check the parameters the system was designed for. Some are better at high rpm while others work well in street situations with relatively low rpm. Make sure that your cam and heads are a good match for the hardware you intend to buy.

Fuel Injection Software

Like the hardware, the basic GM computer and assorted software work pretty well in most situations. For most of us, the stock ECM with a good aftermarket PROM will provide more than enough performance. If your TPI is a speed-density system, then you need to pick a PROM that matches your engine. If it's a mass air system, although it is a little easier, you still need to find a PROM that was designed to work with an engine similar to yours. With a mass air system, the PROM doesn't need to be quite so specific, but even these PROMs are developed for a particular type of engine—in terms of cubic inches, cam, and driving habits.

If you yearn for more power and the ability to program your own fuel and ignition curves, then you need a system like the one from EFI Technology, Haltech, or Motec. With these ECMs and assorted accessories, you can program fuel or

The new LT-1 engine can be run in your street rod wit the help of the right harness and computer from Street & Performance. Note the neat labels, a sign of quality *and a great aid when installing the harness.* Street & Performance

fuel and ignition curves for your engine throughout its operating range. Some, like those from Motec, allow you to fine-tune the curves with a hand-held calibrator while other systems interface with your laptop computer and offer full graphing abilities to help you better visualize engine operation.

These very sophisticated software packages will interface with the stock GM tuned port hardware, or more likely, some kind of aftermarket intake plumbing and manifold. With such systems you don't need a custom PROM "burned" by some computer guru because you are, in essence, burning your own. Want faster warmups? Just specify late ignition timing immediately after startup. If that leaves the engine with too little power, specify late timing for just two cylinders while the others follow a standard ignition map.

Not many street rodders have the inclination (or the money) to step up to this level. But for those who do, the level of control is truly amazing.

Chapter 4

Assembling the Engine–How to Do It Right

No, it may not be the only engine in town, but the small-block Chevy engine is by far the most popular engine used in street rods today. The text that follows discusses disassembly, machine operations, and the assembly of a small-block Chevrolet engine—although most of the operations and procedures would be the same regardless of which brand or type of engine were being repaired.

The first steps in building a great motor are disassembly and degreasing—done in a separate room outside the Wheeler machine shop.

The approach here is realistic. Too many magazine articles are written (book authors are obviously a much better informed bunch of journalists) about high-dollar, high-revving, super-horsepower engines built by well-known shops. The headline proclaims, "Get Six Thousand Horsepower from Your Chevy Small-Block!" It might sell magazines, but if you read the fine print, those 6,000 horses are only available from 8300 to 8500rpm. A Detroit diesel has a broader power band.

The goal for the demonstration engine constructed by Wheeler Racing Engines (and an objective of this book) is to find good horsepower and torque figures obtained at the lower rpm ranges that we encounter on the street. The idea is to construct an engine that will spin the tires when you want to, deliver reasonable mileage, and retain the durability that the small-block is known for. Because the best street rods are the ones that only *look* expensive, we set out to build this engine on a budget.

Inspection

If you're doing the majority of the engine work yourself, then it only makes sense to do the initial disassembly and inspection as well. When you pull the engine apart, make sure all the parts go in boxes and that each box gets labeled.

Many of the parts are going to be discarded in favor of newer, better pieces from the aftermarket. What most builders need most from that old, greasy small-block is a good block, a good crankshaft, a good set of rods, and a good pair of heads.

The block needs to be degreased, of course, with solvent, a series of brushes, and some good hot water. Later, I will recommend another cleaning. If you're doing this at home in the driveway, use a biodegradable soap or solvent for the sake of your lawn and the rest of us. If the engine shop is going to boil the block, then you only need to get things clean enough to inspect the block. Externally, look for frost plugs that have been pushed partway out, meaning the water in the block may have frozen at some time.

Inspection of the parts includes Magnafluxing the crank and rods. First , the part is washed down with a special fluid containing tiny particles of iron.

The part is placed in a magnetic field (created by the loop on Jeff's left), and with the shop light turned off, a black light is turned on. The tiny iron particles will line up in even a miniscule crack, making the crack easy to find.

Frozen water will often crack the block externally, so be sure to look over the sides of the block as well.

Inside, the block needs to be inspected carefully along the valley, just above the lifter bores. Small cracks in this area go into the water jacket, yet they don't leak much water and might have gone unnoticed by the car's last owner. If you have access to inside micrometers, then you can check the bores for overall size and taper. The standard bore size for a 350 Chevy is 4.00in; the ideal block is one that needs only a 0.030in overbore.

You can take your micrometers to the crank journals, but more likely you simply need to give the crank a good visual inspection. Look for damaged journals and obvious signs of use and abuse. The crank will no doubt get a much more thorough inspection by the engine shop or the crank grinding company.

Assuming you are going to use the stock heads, inspecting them for cracks and other flaws is much easier after they've been disassembled and professionally cleaned (see chapter 2 for more information on cylinder heads). With the heads, there isn't much to do except drop them off along with everything else at the engine shop.

Comments made earlier by Jim Petrykowski bear repeating: "I tell 'em to find a good engine shop and then work with the guy who runs that shop. Don't try to weasel the guy out of every nickel. Let the engine shop do what they do best, follow their advice for the kind of engine you want to have—and then save some money by assembling the engine yourself."

Preassembly and Machine Operations

By preassembly, I mean all the things that are done to the engine after the initial inspection—including all the machine operations—and before the final assembly begins.

The importance of Magnafluxing can't be overstated. Crankshafts and connecting rods should always be Magnafluxed to minimize the odds that they will break after you've spent all your time and money building that perfect engine. Parts to be Magnafluxed are first washed down with a special liquid that contains small

After disassembly and inspection, the machine operations begin. On this V-8, the deck has been cut. This provides a good sealing surface for the head, but more importantly it will ensure that the deck surface runs parallel to the crankshaft centerline and that all the cylinders have the same compression ratio.

iron particles. Then the part is placed in a strong magnetic field and the lights are turned off.

With the shop lights turned off, a special black light is turned on (and then we get out the psychedelic posters from 1969 and then...). Any cracks in the metal will upset the magnetic field created in the part and cause the small particles contained in the liquid to collect along the crack. These particles become phosphorescent under the black light—thus a crack in a crankshaft will show up as a line of particles arrayed along the crack. Tiny cracks that were invisible to the naked eye become extremely obvious under the black light.

Machining the Block

Line boring is usually the first machine operation performed on a block to ensure that the crank runs in perfectly aligned bearing caps. Next, the deck, or top surfaces of the block, is cut so its surfaces are perfectly flat and at an angle of 90 degrees to one another.

When it comes to boring the block, most shops cut the bores .030in and install new pistons. At the Wheeler shop and most good engine building shops, the first .025in is removed with the boring bar while the final .005in is removed with the power hone. The honing is done with a torque plate in place across the top surface of the block. This simulates the distortion that occurs when the head is bolted into place, and ensures that the final fit of the pistons is correct.

How far beyond the standard 0.030in cleanup bore you can go depends on the engine family you're working with, the parameters you have set for the project, and the advice of the shop doing the engine work. Some small-block Ford engines, for example, simply don't have enough "meat" in the casting to allow a bore of much more than 0.030in. Art Chrisman is a man who doesn't like to take any more than necessary from an engine during boring. He feels that when the cylinder walls get too thin, they move too much as the engine runs and oil control becomes a problem.

The actual fit of the pistons in the cylinder depends on the type of piston and the use for which the engine is intended. In the case of a Chevy 350 intended for the street using new, forged pistons with high silicone content, the clearance between the piston and the cylinder is 0.0025in. Jeff Fiala at Wheeler Racing took pains to explain that a competition engine using a forged piston with low silicone might run a great deal more than 0.0025in clearance. Each set of pistons comes with a tech sheet regarding the necessary clearance and exactly where the piston should be measured.

If you're building a stock or near-stock motor, then cast pistons might actually be a better answer than forged pistons. Not only do they cost less, but cast pistons allow you to run pretty tight piston-to-cylinder clearances. Hypereutectic is a word heard recently in many engine shops and it describes a special process whereby silicone is introduced and mixed with the casting matrix during the piston-casting process. Hypereutectic is often used to describe a cast piston with a high silicone content.

A small-block bore measures 4.00in stock, so most are bored to a final size of approximately 4.030in (the final size is determined by the dimension of the individual piston). The actual procedure for boring the block and fitting the pistons began with Jeff cutting each cylinder to 4.025in with the boring bar before moving the block to the Sunnen power hone. After mounting the block in the power hone, the torque plate was torqued in place so the cylinder would have ex-

The boring bar is readied for a cut. Each cylinder is cut separately. Ideally you only want to go 0.030in over the stock dimension. In a good shop, the first 0.025in is removed with the bar while the final 0.005in is removed with the power hone.

actly the same shape as after the heads were installed.

Before starting in with the hone, Jeff measured each piston according to the manufacturer's instructions (pistons are not strictly round, so it's important to measure according to the manufacturer's instructions). The clearance between the piston and cylinder is built into the piston. That is, the pistons are something less than the 4.030in dimension of the cylinder. In the case at hand, Jeff wanted a 0.0025in clearance, thus an ideal piston dimension would be 4.0275in. Each piston is measured with a micrometer and any variation from the ideal dimension is noted on the top of the piston in grease pencil. A piston that measures 4.028in, for example, is marked +0.0005 and the cylinder for that piston is honed to 4.0305in. In this way, the fit of each piston is exactly the same throughout the engine.

In the Wheeler shop, most street engines get reconditioned factory connecting rods. Stronger rods can be installed at the customer's request, but Gary Schmidt feels that in most cases they aren't needed. What is needed is a good, reconditioned factory connecting rod.

Before beginning the reconditioning process the rods are Magnafluxed, then checked to make sure they are straight. Rods that pass the first tests get new rod bolts installed before any of the machine operations start. The new bolts, from ARP (Automotive Racing Products) are rated at a tensile strength of 190,000psi, and are carefully pressed into place. A quality shop will inspect the shoulder of the connecting rod where the bolt head rests to make sure the bolt head makes good square contact, and the same is true for the part of the cap that the nuts contact.

Reconditioning begins by resizing the big end of the rod. In essence, the two halves of the rod are ground slightly at their mating surface, then the hole is remachined to the correct size. This results in a perfectly round hole of exactly the right dimension.

The small end is usually checked to ensure that it is the right size. As the piston pin on nearly all small-blocks presses into the small end of the connecting rod, this end must be small enough to ensure a good interference fit. If the

Jeff from Wheeler installs the torque plate. The plate is torqued in place, just like the head, so that the cylinder will have exactly the same shape during the honing that it does in the finished engine.

hole is too big, then the piston pin can work its way to the side until it rubs a groove in the cylinder wall.

More elaborate efforts, like polishing and shot peening the connecting rods, probably aren't necessary for street engines of only modest horsepower.

Crankshafts can be safely turned to any standard undersize, as much as 0.030in less than stock. At the Wheeler shop, the 350 cranks were Magnafluxed and then sent out to a company that does nothing but grind crankshafts. Gary lightly chamfered the oil holes, being careful not to get too carried away.

Balancing

There are at least two reasons to balance your engine before doing the assembly. First, as you add new pistons and/or rods to the crank assembly, the factory balance job is rendered useless. Second, that factory job (even if you ran components of exactly the same weight) was designed for a low-stress street engine that would seldom see high-rpm use.

There are two methods of balancing an engine, internally and externally. Most common is the internally balanced engine like most small-block Chevrolets. (Externally balanced engines include the 400ci small-block and the 454ci big-block.) In the case of internally balanced engines, metal to balance the rotating crankshaft assembly is either added to or subtracted from the counterweights of the crankshaft.

As stated, a good internal balancing job is worth its weight in gold. At the Wheeler shop—or any good shop—the procedure goes like this:

Jeff starts by weighing the large end of each connecting rod on a special scale that weighs one end at a time. After finding the lightest big end, metal is removed from the rectangular pad (the balance pad) on the connecting rod cap of each of the other rods so that all the big ends weigh the same.

The weight of the small end is checked indirectly by checking the total weight of the connecting rods and then removing metal from the balance pad above the small end until all the rods have the same total weight.

After the rods are machined to identical weights, the pistons go through a similar procedure. Jeff finds the lightest one and then removes metal from inside the other seven pistons until they all weigh exactly the same.

Jeff's next task is filling out the bob-weight card. The weight of each component that will attach to the crank—pistons, pins, rods, and bearings—is added together on a bob-weight card. Then four bob weights are assembled with enough lead shot in each one to exactly match the weight of the piston and rod assemblies. These weights—representing the weight of the pistons and rods—are bolted to the crank (see the illustration if this is getting a little fuzzy) and the crank is placed in the balancing machine.

The balancer operates through the use of a strobe light and a small meter. Jeff uses the meter to determine if the crank needs more or less weight, and the light to determine where that weight should be added or subtracted. Adding weight is done by first drilling and then welding in small billets of special, heavy steel. Weight is removed by simply drilling away part of the counterweight.

As the harmonic balancer and flywheel or flexplate are part of the rotating mass of the crankshaft, it's important that they be balanced as well. If the engine uses a manual transmission, then the flywheel should be balanced in two steps: first by itself, and then with the clutch and pressure plate attached.

The cylinders get their final honing and are fit to the pistons with this Sunnen power hone. New pistons are numbered, measured, and marked. Then each cylinder is honed to match the corresponding piston.

Stock rods can be used in a strong street engine, but they must be resized. After grinding material off where the rod cap bolts to the rod, Jeff resizes the big end on this special Sunnen hone.

This scale measures one end of the connecting rod at a time. First, all the big ends are checked and modified so they weigh exactly the same. Then the small ends are equalized to weigh the same amount.

80

This might all seem complex, and it is, but there are a few basic things to keep in mind: If you're building a good engine, spend the money to have it balanced. And once the flywheel and clutch assembly are balanced, they must always be assembled in the same relative positions.

Assembly

The actual assembly of a good engine starts with the block. In the case of the 350 Chevy at the Wheeler shop, Jeff starts with a small grinder to clean up any rough corners in the block which might contain sand and slag that could eventually mix with the oil. Next, the oil return holes at the rear of the valley are chamfered to ensure that the returning oil is not held in the valley during operation. Some shops paint the inside of the block with Rustoleum primer. Jeff explains that at Wheeler, they only paint the inside of the block if the customer requests it or the block itself is very rough and semiporous. In the case of a poor casting, the paint will prevent

any sand from washing out of the block during the engine's life.

After grinding off any rough material inside the block and chamfering the oil return holes, the engine is cleaned one more time. The frost and welch plugs were removed earlier, so it's easy to get inside the water jacket and the oil galleries and get everything very clean.

The smaller welch plug holes that go into the oil galleries and run parallel to the cam, at the front of the engine, are tapped for one-quarter-inch pipe plugs. The tap that Wheeler uses has been cut short so the threads don't go too deep. If the plugs screw in too far, they will actually block off oil in the gallery moving to or from the front cam bearing.

If the engine will run a double-roller timing chain, the builder may need to grind away some of the casting material around the welch plugs at the front of the block to allow clearance for the gear and chain.

Before beginning the actual assembly, Jeff scrubs down the block with cleaning solvent one

The pistons also must be machined to an equal weight. Here, the mill is used to remove metal from inside one of the pistons.

Jeff grinds metal off the balance pad on the bottom of the connecting rod cap. He does this to the seven heaviest rods until they all weigh the same as the lightest one.

more time, and follows up with a good scrubbing using Tide detergent (you may have your own brand preference) in very hot water. He explains that "the solvent seems to lift the material out of the pores of the block, but the Tide actually washes it away." The final step is a good blasting of the block, water jackets, and oil galleries with a high-pressure hose and cool water. The block is dried with compressed air, and then the cylinder bores are wiped down one more time with solvent followed by a wipedown with WD-40 on a towel or rag. WD-40 will pick up any lingering dirt and also prevent rust from forming on the fresh cylinder walls.

If it seems like a lot of washing, remember Jeff's comment that "you can't get them too clean." Cleaning the block also gives the engine builder another opportunity to inspect the block for any problems.

Assembly starts with the installation of new frost plugs. These should be driven in with the appropriate driver, not just a socket on the end of an extension. The driver actually fits the edge of the plugs, rather than putting the force of your hammer against the concave inner part of the plug. Be sure the holes are free of rust and clean; sand the edges of the hole if there's any doubt. Jeff likes to use a nonhardening sealer on the edge of the plugs, like Permatex number two. Do not use silicone on the plugs!

The frost plugs in the side of the block should be driven in until they are flush with the block, particularly the plug at the rear of the block, just behind the last cam bearing. As Jeff reports, "People think that plug goes in until it hits the step farther into the bore but that's too far. When you drive the plug in that far it actually holds the cam forward so the timing chain doesn't run straight and the upper gear rubs on the timing cover."

The preparation of the block always seems to take too long—you might think the job will never end. Yet, when it finally does you can put the engine back in the stand, roll it over, and get ready to lay in the crank.

Jeff recommends that you lay out all the parts before beginning the assembly, to be sure

BOB WEIGHT RECORD	
NAME. Bill Smith	
ENGINE. Chev SIZE. 355	
BORE. _____	RODS. _____
ROTATING ROD.	410
ROTATING ROD.	410
RECIP. ROD.	170
PISTON+PIN.	755
LOCKS.	3
RINGS.	56
INSERTS (2 SETS)	98
OIL	3
TOTAL BOB WT	1905

The weights of all the rotating members are tallied up on this bob-weight card. Then the weights are duplicated and bolted to the crankshaft during the balancing process.

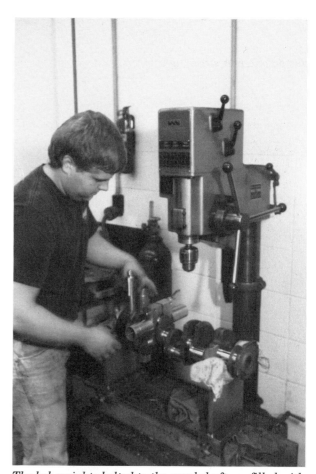

The bob weights bolted to the crankshaft are filled with lead shot until they weigh the same as the piston and rod assemblies.

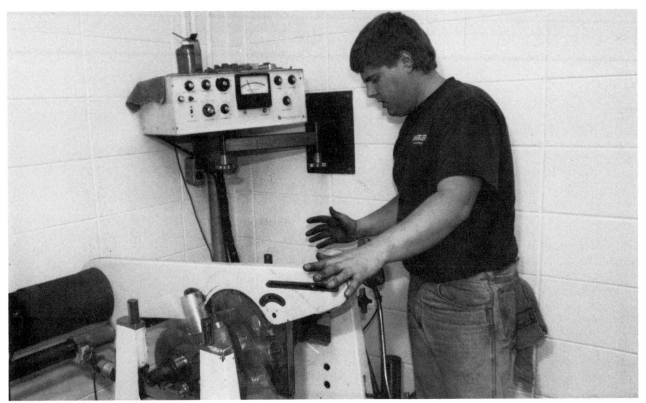

With the bob weights in place, the crankshaft is spun in this balancer. A strobe light behind Jeff's hand shows where the weight needs to be added or removed. The small scale tells him how much to adjust the weight in each case.

Small plugs in the oil galleries were removed earlier for cleaning. Now those galleries are tapped for a tapered pipe plug. Plugs must not go in too far or they can cut off the oil supply to other parts of the engine.

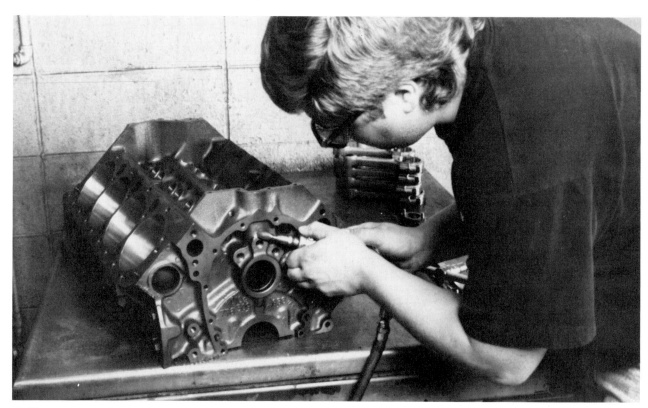

Jeff removes metal near the boss for the oil gallery plug in order to provide clearance for a double-roller timing chain.

Block preparation includes chamfering the oil return openings like the ones in the valley. The idea is to remove any restriction to the oil flow.

they are the right ones and that nothing is packaged incorrectly.

Because cam bearing installation requires a special tool, you might elect to have it done at the engine builder's shop. If you are going to install cam bearings yourself (don't build an engine without putting in new cam bearings), now is the time to do it. It's not uncommon to have a problem with a bearing boss that the factory had to open up after installation to compensate for an incorrectly sized hole in the block. The problem can be easily corrected—if you find it before the entire engine is assembled.

Cam bearings should be installed starting at the rear, and each should be centered in the block opening (in the front-to-rear dimension). After installing the bearings, apply assembly lube to the bearing journals and special camshaft assembly lube to the cam lobes. Then carefully install the cam to avoid nicking the soft cam bearings, and make sure it turns freely without any binding.

Once the cam is installed, it's time to set the crank and bearings in the block. Despite some advice to the contrary, Jeff always washes the new bearings in solvent and gives each one a gentle polishing with an old piece of Scotch-brite.

The oil pump bolts to the rear main cap. Jeff is chamfering the edge of the oil passage in the cap.

The idea is to remove the dirt trapped in the top Babbit coating. This coating is about 0.001in thick, so don't polish off the coating and don't scratch the bearing surface; just polish out the bigger dirt particles trapped there. How-to books have often recommended against removing these dirt particles because people misunderstand the phrase, "Rub each bearing *lightly* with an old worn-out piece of the red Scotch-brite—*don't put any scratches into the actual bearing surface.*" Anyone in doubt about this rub-lightly business should just leave the bearings alone.

Before laying the crank in the new bearings, it's time for some serious cleaning. Grinding and polishing the crank leaves metal chips in the oil passages. The only way to get this material out is with small brushes and large amounts of patience. Long wire and plastic brushes are available at the grocery store or the gun shop (often sold for cleaning gun barrels). Novice builders sometimes experience a bearing failure shortly after starting up a new engine. After teardown, the bearings are found to contain abrasive and metal particles—particles that were trapped inside the crankshaft when the engine was assem-

When all the machine operations and the block preparations are finished, it's time for the final cleaning. Jeff uses cleaning solvent and is careful to get down into all the nooks, crannies, and oil galleries.

A Lifetime of Engines

Gary Schmidt, owner of Wheeler Racing Engines in Blaine, Minnesota, is one of those rare individuals who could see early on what he wanted to do with his life—and lived to do it. His fascination with engines started early and continues to this day. Working with Gary is a little tough because he moves fast and always has about five things going on at any one time. Gary is a man who has built literally thousands of engines of all types. During my time in his shop, I saw everything from small-block Chevys to a 426 wedge Mopar motor. I've always believed that if you want to know how to do something, you should ask the person who does it all day long. Follow along as Gary tells us the dos and don'ts of building a good engine.

Q: *Let's start with a little background on you. Were you always interested in cars and engines? And where did you get your training?*

Gary: I was always into cars and engines. When I was real young I hung around with older car guys. People like Tom Hoover and guys who were really seriously into racing. They let me hang around and they probably took advantage of me to some extent—like getting me to do the nasty dirty jobs and wash a lot of parts. But they taught me a lot. As soon as I got a license, I was into hot rods right away.

Q: *Did you go to trade school, or did you get your early training elsewhere?*

Gary: In high school, I hit it off real well with my teachers. My art teacher let me go down and work in the machine shop during art class. The machine shop instructor liked me because I was real businesslike. I wasn't building knives or screwing off the way a lot of the other kids were. He gave me the run of the shop. I was there for a drafting class, machine shop, and art, so I got to spend four hours every day in the machine shop. I got real good grades and the instructors kind of let me do my own thing.

After high school I went to Dunwoody Institute and took the machinist class. I wanted to build engines and there weren't any good engine machine shop classes at the vo-techs in those days.

About that time I went and talked to Jack Wheeler. Jack's shop [the shop Gary would later buy] was the only place to have a motor built during those days. If you had an engine built by Wheeler, it was a big deal. Jack couldn't hire me at that time, but we hit it off pretty well. Eventually I went to work for Minnesota Auto Specialties, doing fabrication and chassis work.

About a year and a half later, Jack Wheeler put up a new building and then he gave me a call. We talked about a job. He said he wanted someone who would go the distance. He said if I worked there for fifteen years that he would cut me in on the business. Well, after fifteen years, Jack was ready to sell the business. When he did, we kind of figured in the "equity" I'd already earned and now, of course, it's my shop.

Q: *So you knew way back in high school that building motors was what you wanted to do?*

Gary: Yes, in fact I knew before high school. I was always fascinated by engines, in making them go fast, in making them run better and better. Why it works and how it works and how to make it work better.

Q: *What kind of mistakes do people make when they buy or assemble an engine for a street rod?*

Gary: People don't understand the relationship between port volume, runner size, and the rpm range that the cam is designed to run at. They always think bigger ports and a wilder cam will give you more horsepower. They will, but at a much higher rpm than if you ran a smaller cam and smaller ports.

We like to spend a little time with the customer when they come in the door so they don't build an engine—or we don't build it for them—that comes on at 85mph but can't get across the intersection when the light turns green.

Some of the guys won't listen to us—they've read too many magazine articles. They don't really understand how an engine works. The connection between the carb size and cam duration and all the rest. All those parts have to work together and they have to work in the rpm range where the car is going to run. The guys who won't listen, who already know everything, those are the ones who are real hard to work with.

Q: *So, one of the advantages of using a shop like yours is the quality of the advice the customer gets?*

Gary: Yes. I don't want to pick on the big chain-type stores, but they don't hire people with the kind of experience that I do. When you walk into one of those big stores, the guy at the counter will sell you the biggest cam in the catalog because that guy doesn't know—really know—how that cam is going to work with the rest of the components you're going to use in your particular car.

Q: *If I come in to your shop—and other engine building shops where the emphasis is on quality—how do you walk me through the kinds of choices I need to make? How do you make sure I pick the right components for my engine and my car?*

Gary: Well, I start with tire size. We assume that the customer knows what size the rear tires will be. We know that the car should work in that off-idle to 3500rpm range. Not in that over 3500rpm range. So first, I've got to get him to run the right gears, so that the engine rpm at 55 or 60mph is correct.

Q: *Where do you like to see that rpm?*

Gary: I like to see about 2400rpm at highway speeds. That way the car will jump pretty good when you step on the gas, yet it won't be running so many revs that it's real buzzy to ride in. Most street rods are pretty light, so you're not trying to move a lot of weight. If you run a street torque converter that gives an additional 500rpm when you hit the gas, well they'll really come on pretty well when you hit the gas.

Q: *How about budget—how much money does a person have to spend to build a good street rod engine? Something that's dependable and fast, a fairly typical street rod engine.*

Gary: To build an engine in our shop, assuming that the owner doesn't do any of the work him or herself, it will run a little less than $2,000. That includes $200 for the basic core engine. If they assemble the engine themselves, they save about $300 to $350.

That amount includes all the machine work: line bore the block, cut the deck height, bore the cylinders, and then hone the cylinders with a torque plate in place. It includes resized rods with new bolts, new forged pistons, reground and balanced crank assembly, all new bearings of course, and a new cam and new cam bearings.

For the heads, we resurface them, do a complete valve job, and we do a pocket port job. The price also includes things like cleaning the block, new frost plugs, all the gaskets, a new timing chain, a new aluminum intake manifold, and cutting that intake manifold if it's necessary.

Q: *Do people try to skimp and save a buck? And what are the problems that arise as a result of that?*

Gary: Too many guys try to reuse the pistons. They think they're going to be able to use those pistons again, in a motor that's got a lot of miles on it. It doesn't work; there are just certain things you have to do to do it right, to have a real good engine. And they want to skip the balance, which is only a little more than a hundred bucks. To me, in a street rod engine, there's nothing more impressive than a real smooth engine. The balance really makes a difference and it doesn't cost too much and it's foolish to skip that part of it.

Q: *Talk about the basics of the engine building process. How far can you bore a block, and how much can you take off the crankshaft and still have good quality parts?*

Gary: If you're talking about a 350 Chevy engine, the cylinder walls are pretty consistent. You want to keep the bore as small as possible, for strength, to keep the heat in the cylinder and so the cylinder walls aren't moving when the engine runs.

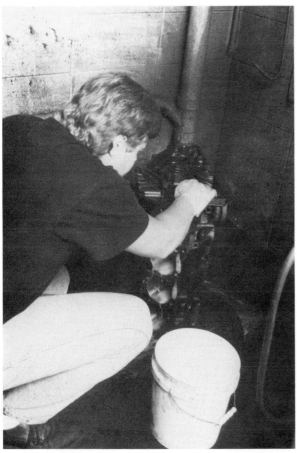

Next, Jeff washes the block down again with soap and water. This tends to lift any lingering dirt from the block and cylinder surfaces.

Now is a good time to clean the crank as well. Turning and polishing leaves abrasives and metal chips in the oil galleries. All those impurities must be removed before the engine is assembled.

Most off-the-shelf performance pistons only come in 0.030 and 0.060in over. So you've really got to run 0.030 over—and the small-block will do it just fine—but I don't like to run any more than that.

Other motors are harder to bore. Ford small-blocks, for example, have thinner walls and less consistent castings than do Chevrolets. People who build a Ford often buy a number of blocks and then sonic test each one to find out which has the best bores, the most consistent casting. So you spend more time and more money on one of those engines.

For the crankshaft, we've never had a problem in our shop with using the common undersizes available. There isn't any real loss of strength. When they regrind a crank, they do a better job [than the factory] of grinding the radius on the journals and that helps to keep the shaft from cracking.

Generally if a crankshaft is really badly damaged and will need more than 0.010in to clean it up, there's probably other damage to the crank as well. Most of those are discarded along the way before they get reground. I don't have a problem with having a crank that's already 0.010in under reground to the next undersize if the only problem is wear.

Q: *What about all the people who say, "I ran a thirty-under crank in my car once and it failed right away"?*

Gary: The reason it failed is that the crank wasn't the only thing that was damaged. If you damage the crank so bad it won't clean up until you've got it thirty-under, well there's probably damage to other parts as well. The bearing probably spun, so there's probably damage to the main saddle or the big end of the rod. When you spin a rod, it creates heat and distortion to the saddle or big end that holds the bearing. If it was a rod that spun, then the rod should be resized, if it was a main, then it should be line bored. But these guys don't do that, they just put the reground crank in and then it fails and they blame it on the crankshaft being thirty-under.

Q: *What about cross-drilled cranks for the street, and what about chamfered oil holes?*

Gary: You really don't need cross-drilled [or full-time oiling] on the street, it just isn't necessary. As for the oil holes, we break the surface where the hole hits the journal, but we don't really try to open that hole up. I've seen people get carried away with that and it reduces the available bearing surface.

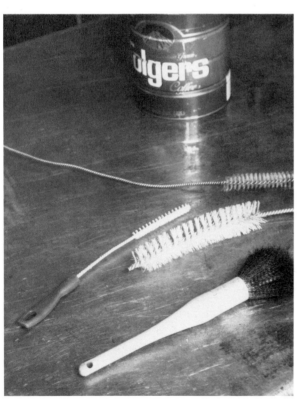

Small brushes like these work well for cleaning the galleries in the crank and also the nooks and crannies in the block. They can be purchased at a grocery, hardware store, or gun shop.

When you're all finished, you've got a gleaming engine block like this one. All the machine operations have been performed, and you're ready to install internal engine parts.

First, put a little sealer around the lip of the new frost plugs and then drive them in with the correct driver.

bled. So be sure to clean the crank thoroughly. The final step in crankshaft cleaning is blowing out the passages with compressed air.

You might think we're finally ready to set that crank into the block. Well, there's just one more thing. The correct way to install a bearing is to set the side with the locking lip into the recess and then push on the other side of the bearing so it snaps into place. As the bearing is pushed past the edge of the bearing cap or recess, there is a chance that a burr on the edge of the block or the cap will peel metal off the back of the bearing. To prevent this, Jeff takes a fine abrasive pad and sands the edge of the cap to eliminate any rough or sharp edges that will catch on the backside of the bearing as it slides past.

I should note that the main and rod bearings come with some "spread" intended to keep them tight against the bearing cap or recess. People sometimes set the bearing into the recess and then push on the center of the bearing with their thumb until it is forced into place. This is incorrect, and will collapse the bearing and eliminate the crush that is designed into every bearing.

A good assembly lube should be used on all bearing surfaces—such as heavy engine oil or STP Oil Treatment or a lube specifically designed to provide lubrication to the bearings—until the oil pump is primed and pumping oil throughout the engine. Jeff and Gary Schmidt from Wheeler recommend against products like white lithium or moly lube (often used as a chassis lube).

Before dropping in the crankshaft, install the top half of the rear seal (pre-1987 small-blocks) using a light coating of sealer behind the seal. Most shops offset the seal slightly so the two halves of the seal don't line up with the split where the main cap bolts to the block. Some shops remove the little oil-diverter plug that sits in a gallery on top of the rear main cap (see the illustration for clarification). Be sure this plug is in place before installing the crank and rear main cap.

Now, after installing the top half of all the bearings, you can set the crank into the block. Jeff likes to install the bearing caps for the front four bearings, torque them down in two steps, and then check the end play of the crankshaft.

This cam plug at the back of the block should be installed flush with the block—not pushed into the first step inside the bore.

A tapered, threaded plug is installed in the oil gallery—instead of the factory plug.

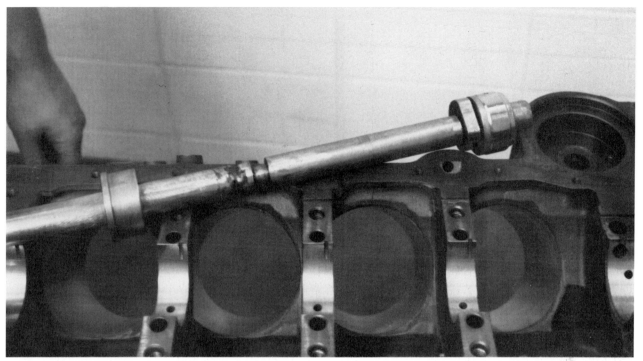

This special tool is designed for installing cam bearings. The cam and bearings should be installed before the rest of the internal parts in case there's any irregularity in the size of the bearing bores.

Jeff installs the cam bearings, starting at the rear of the engine and working toward the front.

Before installing the cam and bearings, the journals are coated with assembly lube. The lobes themselves get special lube designed for the high loads encountered by the cam and lifters.

Like the bearings, the bearing caps are set down on one side and then tapped lightly on the opposite side (tapping toward the center of the crankshaft) until the bearing cap is fully seated in the block. Yes, people have been known to torque bearing cap bolts without making sure the cap was fully seated—breaking the bearing cap into two pieces in the process.

With four main caps installed and no prelube of any kind on the thrust surface of the rear bearing, Jeff installs a dial indicator and then takes a reading of crankshaft end play (end play on a small-block should read 0.003 to 0.006in). After getting the initial reading, Jeff installs the bearing cap for number five main bearing, snugs the bolts, and takes another reading. Ideally, the second reading should match the first. If it's a couple of thousandths inch less, the number five bearing cap can be moved ever so slightly to try and align the bearing cap with the bearing in the block.

When the end play reading is correct, the last main cap can be torqued down and the thrust surface can be lubricated with engine oil alongside the main cap. The crankshaft should turn freely now, without any bind. If there is bind in the shaft, don't expect it to wear in; call the shop that did the machine work and ask them for help.

The cam is installed carefully, so as not to nick the soft bearings.

Before installing rings on pistons and pistons in cylinders, the end gap of the rings must be checked. Gary and Jeff use a specification of 0.004in per inch of piston diameter for the top ring and 0.003in per inch for the second ring. All the rings are laid out per the cylinder they go in. Then Jeff pushes each ring down into the cylinder partway, using an old flat-top piston to be sure the rings are positioned square in the bore, and checks the end gap. Small, special grinders are available for filing the end gap, or a small file can be used. After removing metal in the fixture, Jeff removes any burrs with a small pumice stone.

Before putting the rings on the pistons, Jeff presses the piston pins into the pistons and rods using a small press and the correct driver. Because the bottom end of the rods were assembled so they could be resized, the rod cap must now be separated from the rod itself. This may sound like no big deal, yet performing this little task without damaging the connecting rod is tougher than it seems.

Jeff mounts the rod and piston assembly in a vise with aluminum jaws, being sure to grab the connecting rod by the bearing cap, and then uses a punch and hammer on each connecting rod bolt to carefully push the connecting rod apart.

The bore under the rear main cap, where the small oil diverter plug goes. Be sure this plug is in place, as it's sometimes removed during the block cleaning.

Dirt is polished out of the new bearings—without removing the flash coating or scratching the surface.

Jeff installs the rings on each piston, starting with the oil ring and moving up the piston. He notes, "It's real important that the rings go on the right way. For example, the second ring is really just an oil scraper. It's tapered so that one edge scrapes the cylinder wall as the piston moves down. If you put that ring on upside down, it moves the oil up toward the combustion chamber rather than down toward the oil pan. Each brand of ring has its own makings, so you have to be sure to follow the manufacturer's recommendations."

After installing piston rings, each piston and cylinder is oiled lightly with 5W-30 oil. Jeff puts only a light coat on the pistons, rings, and cylinder walls; he feels that's an adequate amount. Before pushing each piston into the proper cylinder, special rubber covers are rolled over each rod bolt. Think of these as "bolt condoms" that ensure safe passage of the rod bolts past the crankshaft journals without nicking those journals. In a pinch, a piece of neoprene gas line can be used to cover the rod bolts.

A ring compressor is then wrapped around the rings and each piston is tapped lightly into the cylinder. Remember that if the going gets tough, the tough (or at least the smart) pull the piston back out of the cylinder and start over. You don't want to break a ring or score a cylinder wall just because you were in too big a hurry.

Installation of the timing chain and gears is next. As was mentioned earlier, if you're using a double-roller chain some metal will have to be removed from the area around the upper oil gallery plug. In some cases, there is raised lettering in the area where the upper gear runs that will interfere as well.

The normal procedure is to install the two gears so the top notch is at the bottom and the bottom notch is at the top (on the small gear). In order to check the precise timing of the camshaft relative to the crankshaft, it's necessary to "degree" the engine with a degree wheel. The idea is to find the high point of the intake lobe (known as the intake lobe centerline) and its relation to

To install the bearings, set the end with the tang into place and then press on the other side of the bearing until it snaps into place.

It's a good idea to remove any rough edges on the cap or block where the bearing slides past, to avoid raising any burrs on the backside of the bearing itself.

crankshaft rotation. It's not as tough as it sounds. The procedure is as follows:

Once the timing chain is on the engine, install the degree wheel on the crank and find a good location for the pointer. (See the illustration for help.)

First, you need to find TDC (top dead center). So, using the dial indicator on the number one piston, find the approximate location of TDC. (It's hard to find precisely because the piston hangs at the top for a few degrees while the crank goes up to and past TDC.) To find the exact location of TDC start with the approximate location, then rotate 0.050in before, and mark the degree wheel. Then go 0.050 past TDC in the other direction and mark that spot. Split the difference between the two marks and use that location as TDC.

Now put the dial indicator on the intake lobe for number one cylinder. Run the lobe to the top as best you can tell and mark that position on the degree wheel. Then go 0.050 in either direction (as you did with the TDC determination) and use the center of those two marks as the intake lobe centerline. You can determine how

many crankshaft degrees that centerline is from TDC and compare that to the information that came with the camshaft. A difference of only a few degrees isn't worth worrying about. If the difference between your readings and the specs approaches ten degrees, you will have to take action in the form of a special lower gear, a slotted cam gear, or offset cam bushings.

At this point the short-block is nearly complete. The crank is installed, as are the pistons, camshaft, and timing gears. The next operation is the installation of the oil pump. The pump Jeff installed was a new pump from Melling. Considering the modest cost of a new pump, it doesn't make sense to use the old one. On small-blocks meant for the street, Wheeler installs a standard volume pump with the high-pressure (Z-28) bypass spring.

Jeff mounts the pump on the engine, sets the new pickup in place, and then measures the height from the bottom of the block. (Be sure to compensate for the thickness of the pan gasket) to the bottom of the pickup. He compares this measurement to the depth of the oil pan and adjusts the pickup to ride about one-half inch or

Bearings are in place, as is the two-piece rear seal (which was used until 1986). Note that the seal is turned slightly so the two halves do not line up with bearing cap surface.

slightly less from the bottom of the oil pan. People sometimes check the measurement with a piece of clay, but if you measure carefully and compensate for the thickness of the gasket, the double-check shouldn't be necessary.

There are a couple of additional steps before you're finished with the oil pump. First, the pick-up is tack welded to the pump so that it will not fall off or move during operation. Finally, the pump cover is removed and the pump is filled with oil (not grease) so it will prime easily the first time the engine is turned over.

Once the bottom end is bolted together, it's time to install the heads. In most cases the heads have been planned to ensure they are perfectly smooth. Gary and Jeff use composition head gaskets (a metal gasket with fiber bonded to either side of the metal). Most of the new gaskets are coated with some kind of a sealer or bonding agent, thus Gary and the crew do not use any additional sealer on the head gaskets.

Gary torques the heads down in three stages, following the correct tightening sequence, and then double-checks the final torque of all the head bolts.

Once the heads are bolted to the block, it's time to install and adjust the valvetrain. Jeff took over this part of the operation and started by screwing the rocker studs into the heads. The heads were modified earlier (see chapter 2) for these studs, which are considered stronger and less prone to flexing during operation than the studs used by the factory. These studs are exposed to water on the bottom side, thus each is coated with sealant (like Permatex number one) and then torqued to 55lb-ft.

Next, the lifters are set in their bores. The lifter bores and sides are coated with assembly lube or engine oil while the bottoms are generously coated with cam lube or moly lube. Jeff points out that sometimes builders coat the body of the lifter with moly lube. "But it's not a good idea to put that heavy lube on the sides of the lifter because then the lifter can't rotate in the bore, and if it can't rotate, it will wear the hell out of the cam lobe."

Before dropping the pushrods into place, both ends should be dipped in oil. If you are using the old pushrods, roll them across the bench to make sure that none of them are bent.

Before dropping the crank in place, Jeff pre-lubes all the bearings.

The balanced crankshaft is carefully set in place.

Bearing caps are set in on one side, then tapped carefully until the other side drops into the register of the block.

The thrust bearing cap and the other half of the rear seal. The seal is installed to match the offset of the other half installed in the block. A bit of sealer is applied to the backside of the seal. Always check the crank end play during assembly.

Stock type rockers like those used in the demonstration engine should have moly lube applied to the pivot ball, as it can take oil quite awhile to work its way up to the rocker arms after startup.

When it comes to adjusting the valves on a small-block with hydraulic lifters, everyone seems to know the "best" way, and no two methods are exactly the same. Jeff and Gary have been building engines for a number of years, and their way goes as follows:

Once all the rockers are loosely installed, Jeff puts number one cylinder on TDC of the compression stroke and then runs the rocker nut down to roughly zero lash, leaving it a little loose. Then he runs all the nuts down the same amount on their studs.

I should point out that these were standard, anti-pump-up hydraulic lifters, installed out of the box and not pre-oiled in any way.

With number one cylinder still at TDC of the compression stroke, Jeff adjusts the rocker nuts for those two valves to zero lash—so there is no up-and-down movement in the pushrod, though the hydraulic lifter has not bottomed out. Then

he turns each nut an additional 180 degrees. Because all eight cylinders will fire in two complete revolutions, each quarter turn of the crank will put the next cylinder in the firing order up on TDC of its compression stroke (two turns divided by eight equals one-quarter). So he turns the crank one-quarter turn at a time (watching the cam action to reinforce that the right cylinder was coming up on TDC) and adjusts the valves for each cylinder in the firing order.

Installing the intake manifold might be another one of those operations that seem too simple to worry about. Yet, Jeff and Gary report that they get a lot of questions from people who assembled their engine only to find that they either smoke or idle at 3000rpm—because the manifold didn't seal along the bottom or the top.

Gary developed a procedure for installing intake manifolds after years of running a supercharged engine at the drag strip. As Jeff explains, "If you can get the intake gaskets to hold in a supercharged engine, well then you must be doing something right."

End gaps must be checked before installing all top and second piston rings.

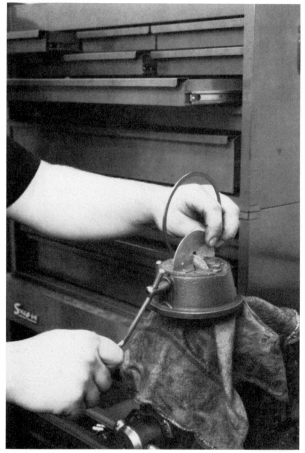

This small grinder is specially designed to open up the piston ring end gaps.

First, before installing any gaskets, the manifold is set down on the otherwise assembled engine. Due to flaws in intake castings and the effects of shaving cylinder heads, the intake may not match up correctly with the cylinder heads. So Jeff and Gary start with a good visual inspection of those surfaces. Is there good contact at all gasket surfaces, are the angles the same and do all the bolt holes line up? It's easier to machine the manifold at this point than it is to fight a vacuum leak later.

After checking the match between the intake manifold and the heads, Jeff glues the paper type intake gaskets (not the steel type) to the head surfaces. On the end rails Jeff uses a bead of silicone. Before setting on the manifold, he coats the paper gaskets with light engine oil. This allows the manifold to settle easily onto the gaskets and find its own ideal position.

Once the intake manifold is set in place, Jeff checks again to be sure all the bolt holes line up. The bolts should line up and start without any Herculean efforts with the pry bar. Under the head of each intake bolt, Jeff uses a heavy, slightly cupped washer. The special shape (the concave side should face up) allows the manifold to move slightly as the bolts are tightened. The tightening sequence starts from the center and works from side to side toward the ends like a cylinder head.

Before the piston rings can be installed, the connecting rods must be disassembled (they are assembled during the resizing process). Jeff has carefully clamped the bearing cap in the vise with the aluminum jaws, and taps carefully on the rod bolts to pry the connecting rod apart.

It might seem like a lot of work for something as simple as installing an intake manifold, but when you're done the manifold will be installed correctly and you won't be trying to trace mysterious oil or vacuum leaks.

Well, there isn't much left to do before we test fire and dyno the demonstration engine (see chapter 2). Valve cover gaskets (cork in this case) are glued in to the covers with 3M Weather Strip Adhesive, using no sealer between the gasket and the head surface. Then the carburetor and water pump are added and this mighty small-block is ready to run.

Conclusion

You don't have to use the most expensive parts to build a good engine. You *do* need to use quality parts mixed with some common sense. If the budget is tight, then use cast pistons, but buy good ones from a reputable supplier. And when you don't know something, don't be afraid to ask. Make sure the people you ask have the credentials and experience to back up their opinions. This all becomes a lot easier if you can find a

This special tool carefully opens the piston ring so it can slide down onto the piston, thus avoiding breakage of the somewhat fragile rings.

The pistons are laid out in order with their bearing caps before being installed into the motor.

100

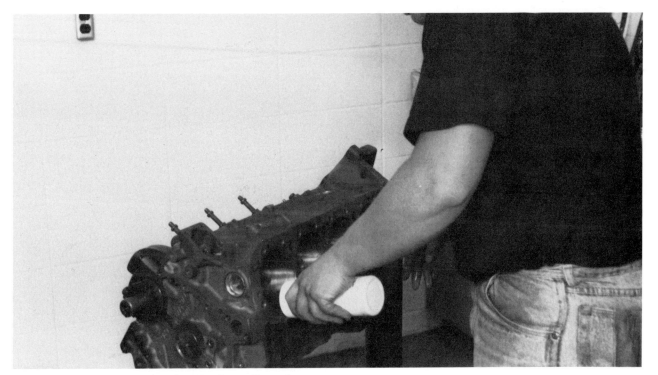

Jeff puts a coating of oil on the cylinder walls and on the pistons and rings before pushing the pistons down into the cylinders.

When installing the pistons it's important to tap carefully, stopping if too much resistance is felt.

Rod caps are installed in the same position they were in before resizing. Jeff snugs the caps with the speed wrench.

The connecting rod caps are torqued to factory specs. Like the main bearings, these caps were coated with lube before assembly.

good engine shop to work with and if you treat that shop as your partner in the process of building a good engine for your new hot rod.

The dial indicator is used to find the centerline of the cam lobe. That centerline is marked on the degree wheel and compared to the specs that came with the camshaft.

A little red Loctite is installed on the cam bolts—after the timing is checked with a degree wheel.

It's a good idea to make sure that true TDC matches up with the timing marks on the outside of the engine.

At the Wheeler shop, engines always get a new oil pump. Here we see the two springs, the stock spring, and the higher pressure (Z-28) spring that were used in the engine.

Jeff checks the clearance between the gears and the cover. If it's excessive, the oil pressure won't be up to snuff. The body of the pump can be machined to decrease the clearance.

Before bolting the cover on the oil pump, it's filled with oil to ensure that it will prime and pump right away when the engine is turned over the first time.

Jeff concentrates mightily on the correct height for the pump pickup. The pickup is tack welded in place before final assembly to make sure it doesn't move.

Gary sets the cylinder heads in place. The intake gaskets have already been glued into place—usually the *manifold would be test fitted first before gluing the gaskets in place.*

Gary torques the heads down in three steps.

Camshaft assembly lube is applied to the lifter bottoms where they ride on the cam—but not on the sides.

Jeff puts a coating of oil on each end of the new pushrods as they are installed.

The paper intake gaskets have been glued to the head. Jeff oils the gasket surface so the intake can slide down into place.

A bead of silicone sealer is used at the end rails between the intake and the block.

After carefully setting the intake in place and bolting it down, the engine is nearly completed and ready for some testing on the dyno.

Chapter 5

Selecting a Transmission

The drivetrain on your rod is made up of three basic components: the engine, transmission, and rear end. Choosing a transmission might seem the easiest part of the deal—whatever came attached to the rear of the used engine you brought home must be the right one, right? Actually, it's not that easy because there are more transmission choices now than ever before.

To Shift or Not to Shift

Before deciding which transmission to run, you need to decide which type of transmission to install. Will this be a shift or a "shift-less" car (as my mother used to say). The decision is a personal one. At any show, the automatics outnumber the sticks by about five hundred to one. The reasons aren't too hard to figure out, either.

Most late-model engines are equipped for an automatic transmission; an automatic may have

If you want to shift your street rod, then you need a standard transmission and some type of clutch linkage. This Doug Nash (now known as Richmond Gear) five- *speed is ready to install in Dennis Varni's Model A roadster.*

been part of the package when you bought the engine. And besides, if you run an automatic you won't have to bother with designing and installing clutch linkage.

A car with a four- or five-speed manual transmission often costs more and involves more work. This is not to say it isn't worth the trouble. Street rods seem like cars that are meant to be *driven* (in spite of all the cruising that most of us do). Driving a car means controlling the car, and a car with a manual shift sure seems like one that you drive rather than just point.

Besides, there's something kind of elemental, invigorating, and sexy about that chrome shift lever coming up out of the floor. The vibrations run up through the stick into your right hand as the motor zooms past 3000rpm and quickly heads for redline. Your right arm tingles as your brain tells you to anticipate that first shift. Bang, you're in second gear, the car takes a leap forward, and it all starts over again.

As I stated, choosing between a manual and an automatic transmission is a personal decision, and one that shouldn't be passed off lightly.

The housing on the input shaft is the hydraulic slave cylinder. There are a variety of master-slave cylinder combinations available, some from companies like JFZ, better known for their brake components.

Installed in the Model A, the five-speed has a nice, low first gear and is still able to cruise comfortably on the highway. Of note, this transmission is now available with six speeds.

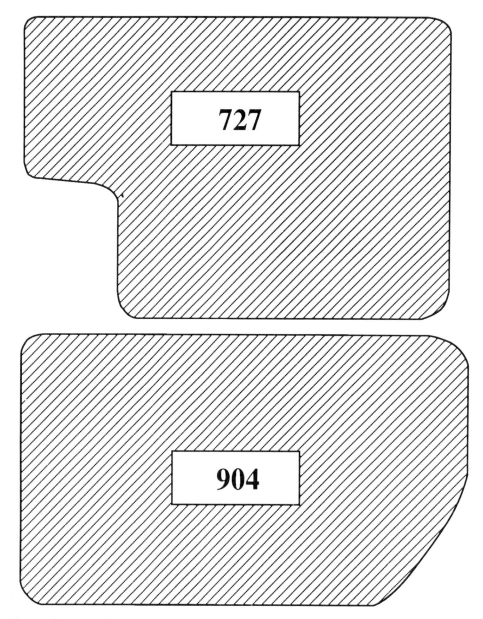

CHRYSLER TORQUEFLITE APPLICATIONS
The lighter duty 904 Torqueflite was used behind both the 6 cylinder engines and some small-block engines. The 904 was not used behind the big-block family of engines.

The heavy duty 727 was used by Chrysler with all three engine families:
* Six cylinder taxis and other heavy duty use.
* High performance small-blocks, like 340 Dodge Darts and 383ci Barracudas.
* Big-block applications from 361 and 383ci sedans to high performance 440 Road Runners.

The easiest way to tell the difference between a 727 and a 904 is the shape of the pan.

Here's the difference between the Chrysler Torqueflite applications: The lighter-duty 904 Torqueflite was used behind both the 6-cylinder engines and some small-block engines. The 904 was not used behind the big-block family of engines. Chrysler used the heavy duty 727 with all three engine families, including: 6-cylinder taxis and other heavy duty uses; high-performance small-blocks such as the 340 Dodge Dart and 383ci Barracudas; and big-block applications from 361ci and 383ci sedans to high-performance 440ci Road Runners.

If you wonder how much torque the 700 R4 can handle, check out this example behind a four-cam ZR-1 Corvette motor.

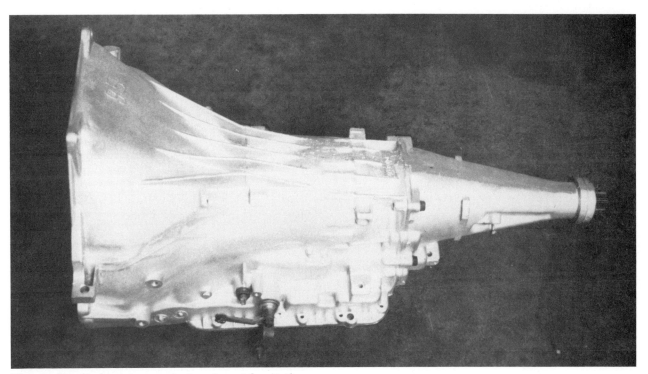

This is Ford's best transmission (or at least the strongest), the C6. The ribbing on the bell housing provides added strength.

Choosing the Right Automatic Transmission
General Motors

The most popular transmission in the GM line is the Turbo Hydra-Matic 350. Built from 1969 to 1979 and from 1980 to 1984 in a lock-up version, there are literally millions of these transmissions out there in the bone yards of America. The 350 is relatively small and short, it's easy to find parts for, and it will handle all but the most powerful engines.

The earlier, pre-lock-up versions of the 350 are the most desirable. (For more insights on the 350 transmission, see John Sevelius' comments later in this chapter.) Most 350 housings are the same, although some heavy-duty truck applications featured a reinforced housing.

In terms of length, the main housings are all the same; any difference in length from one 350 to another is in the tailshaft housings. The most common tailshaft housings measure either 6 or

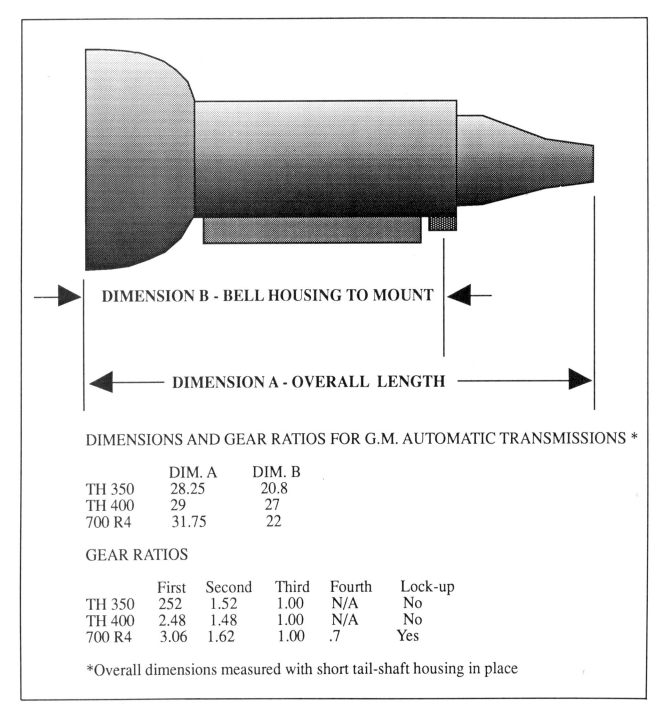

DIMENSION B - BELL HOUSING TO MOUNT

DIMENSION A - OVERALL LENGTH

DIMENSIONS AND GEAR RATIOS FOR G.M. AUTOMATIC TRANSMISSIONS *

	DIM. A	DIM. B
TH 350	28.25	20.8
TH 400	29	27
700 R4	31.75	22

GEAR RATIOS

	First	Second	Third	Fourth	Lock-up
TH 350	252	1.52	1.00	N/A	No
TH 400	2.48	1.48	1.00	N/A	No
700 R4	3.06	1.62	1.00	.7	Yes

*Overall dimensions measured with short tail-shaft housing in place

The inside of a 350 Turbo Hydro. Heavy-duty components can be added to build a 350 that will handle all but the most severe abuse.

10in long. Overall length of a 350 with the short housing is just over 28in from the edge of the bell housing to the end of the tailshaft housing. The location of the rear mount is not affected by your choice of tailshaft housings because the rear mount bolts to the main transmission case—not the tailshaft housing.

There is one other difference in the various tailshaft housings, and that is the diameter of the speedometer drive housing. Early transmissions carried a speedo housing that was only about 1in in diameter where it passed through the tailshaft housing (see photos for clarification). Later housings have a much larger hole and speedo housing, more than double the size of the earlier speedometer gear housing.

In hooking up a 350 transmission in your street rod, you will need shift linkage and a vacuum line to the modulator, to control the shift points and shift quality.

The Turbo Hydra-Matic 400 might be called a heavy-duty transmission, often offered in high-horsepower cars and in many GM trucks. The transmission is slightly larger in diameter, heav-

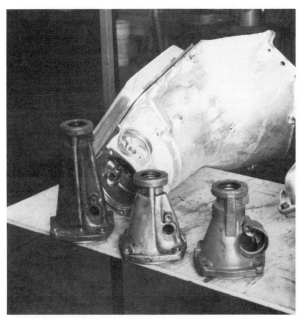

A look at a 350, and the three most common tailshaft housings. Note the difference in diameter where the speedo drive slides in.

ier, and longer by 1in than the 350 transmission, and its rear mount bolts to the tailshaft housing. If you've got a lot of horsepower on tap and intend to really pound on the car, then the Turbo Hydro 400 might be the answer. As with the smaller 350, you need shift linkage and a vacuum line to the vacuum modulator.

From 1965 to 1967, GM offered an interesting version of the Turbo Hydro 400 transmission. Known as the switch-pitch 400, this transmission used a stator (the vaned unit positioned between the drive and driven members of the torque converter) with pivoting vanes. In essence, the angle of the vanes could be changed from a high-stall speed for acceleration to a low-stall speed for efficient highway cruising.

The switch-pitch 400 makes a good street rod transmission, though it might be hard to find. These transmissions were offered in Buicks, Oldsmobiles, Cadillacs, and Rolls-Royces during the two-year period. If you can't find one, call RDS Specialties Incorporated in LeSueur, Minnesota, for a complete transmission or a kit to convert your conventional 400 transmission to the switch-pitch design.

In the early 1980s GM used a 200 R4 automatic transmission. These are not modified 350s and are not part of the 700 R4 line. GM had a lot of trouble with these units, and you're probably better off to avoid using one of these transmissions.

Introduced in 1982, the 700 R4 transmission is a true four-speed transmission with a lock-up torque converter. This transmission allows you to "have your cake and eat it too."

First gear is low—3.06:1—for a good launch, yet the fourth-gear ratio is an overdrive—7:1—for a nice, easy-cruising rpm even with a relatively deep set of rear gears. This is truly the best of both worlds.

Though the transmission earned a bad reputation for durability during its first years on the street, those troubles are in the past. A standard R4 can handle up to 325lb-ft of torque and the factory performance versions can handle up to 375lb-ft. Aftermarket suppliers and specialty shops can modify the R4 to handle as much as 500lb-ft and 700hp.

Though most R4s fit all late-model small-blocks, some were designed for the metric bolt

The inside of a Turbo Hydro 400 torque converter. The four basic components are the housing, impeller, tur- *bine, and stator (the small unit in the center). Shape of the vanes determines the stall speed.*

pattern. Be sure the two upper mounting holes measure 8.25in from center to center.

The R4s built after 1987 are superior to earlier units (these have pressure ports on the rear of the housings while the earlier models do not),although the earliest R4s can be upgraded with the latest parts. If the transmission you're using is four or five years old, it's probably not a bad idea to have it overhauled before installation anyway. If it's an early model, the transmission shop can upgrade it to the latest specifications and install heavy-duty clutches at the same time.

As the 700 R4 continues to grow in popularity (and availability), a lot of people will consider converting their ride from a 350 to a 700 R4. The task isn't too tough, but there are a few sticky points.

First, even though the two transmissions are roughly the same size (with a short tailshaft housing on the 350) the R4 is longer by 3 1/2in. In particular, the R4 has a pan that comes back about 2in farther, so the rear cross-member must allow clearance for this longer pan. The rear mount on an R4 is located about 1in farther back (measured from the front of the bell housing) than on a 350. Other differences include the need for the black box or computer on the R4 to control shifting, and the elimination of the vacuum line to the modulator. When you install an R4 in place of a 350, you need to hook up a throttle cable to the accelerator linkage.

The new throttle cable includes an adjustment on the upper end (the end near the carburetor). The adjuster is a spring-loaded brass button. John Sevelius from Metro/Matic Transmission cautions that a lot of transmissions are ruined due to incorrect adjustment of this cable. He recommends the following procedure for the initial adjustment. First, with the cable hooked up on both ends, a helper under the hood must press the brass button and hold it depressed (this releases the cable housing). Second, a helper in the car must floor the accelerator. Third, while the accelerator is floored, the button must be released. Small adjustments can be made to fine-tune the shifts and shift points to your liking.

A look inside the 700 R4 lock-up torque converter. The two halves of the housing seen on the left form the "clutch" for lock-up. Normally there is no way to check *this clutch, thus the torque converter should always be replaced with a rebuilt converter when the transmission is overhauled.*

This is the front pump and pump housing from an R4. An electronic solenoid controls oil flow within the transmission, which in turn controls the lock-up function.

The two most common tailshaft housings for the 700 R4 are shown here, along with the two sizes of speedometer housings used with various GM automatic transmissions.

FoMoCo

Ford offers three basic automatics, the C4, C6, and the new AOD (Automatic Overdrive) automatic. While the C4 is fine for small-blocks of modest power, the C6 is a much stronger transmission. Although it's an older design, parts for the C6 are still readily available.

The AOD is used behind current Ford small-blocks, including 5.0 liter Mustangs. Like the 700 R4, this is a true four-speed transmission with a lock-up torque converter.

Mopar

If you need an automatic behind a Chrysler Corporation engine, then there's only one answer and it's a good one. The Torqueflite is a great design, produced in two versions: the 904 and the 727. The 727 is by far the superior unit from a standpoint of strength; however, a 904 will work just fine with small-blocks of reasonable power. In size the two transmissions are very similar, with the 727 being a bit thicker through the center of the housing. The 727 can be built to street hemi specs and beyond—this is a very durable transmission.

At one time or another, the 727 has been bolted up behind nearly all the Chrysler engines (see the chart for a breakdown of various applications).

Conclusion

Before bolting in the new (or old) transmission, there are a few things to keep in mind. When in doubt, spend the bucks and have the transmission overhauled. John Sevelius tells me that not all rebuilt transmissions are the same, so be sure to buy from a reputable rebuilder. Even if the used transmission you bought was sold as a "good one," at least change the fluid and filter before you run the car the first time. And remember to give it regular fluid and filter changes once it's in service, the same as you do your daily driver.

Remember, too, that the clutch in a lock-up torque converter can't be checked because it's sealed inside the converter. The only way to be sure the clutch is good is to buy a rebuilt converter.

Automatic transmissions that fail prematurely usually do so because of excessive heat. If you intend to run 'er hard, then install an aftermarket transmission cooler—this will also take that additional heat load off the radiator and allow it to do a better job of cooling the motor. It also means you don't have to find a radiator with a cooler built into the bottom tank.

The 700 R4 on the left has an oil pan about 2in longer than the 350 on the right. The rear mount on the R4 is about 1in farther back than the mount on the 350.

Highly Recommended: An Expert's Views on Transmissions for Your Rod

John Sevelius, owner of Metro/Matic Transmission, White Bear Lake, Minnesota, is an avid street rodder, hot rodder, and fan of custom cars. His "new" ride is a '35 Chevy cabriolet equipped with a big-block and a Turbo Hydro 350 transmission, though he recently sold a 1953 Ford Vicky done as a mild custom. John runs the shop with his son Randy, and his daughter Donna keeps the books. John reports that in the spring and summer, nearly all their work comes from street rodders, restorers, and builders of unusual automobiles. After more than a quarter century of experience with automatic transmissions, John has a few comments regarding the automatic you put in that new street rod.

Q: *John, how long have you been repairing and overhauling automatic transmissions?*

John: I've been doing this for thirty-three years. I'm not sure I know anything else.

Q: *Tell me a little bit about the two most popular automatics from a street rodder's perspective—the Turbo Hydro 350 and the 400. When should a person use the bigger and presumably stronger 400? How much power can be run through the 350?*

John: Well, there's more than one version of the 350. If you buy a 350, buy one that was manufactured before 1980. In 1980 they went to a lock-up torque converter and it just isn't a very good design. Actually, you probably won't find any of those transmissions because most of them have been converted to the pre-1980 style without the lock-up feature.

I'm a big believer in the 350. We built one for my Chevy and it's got a 470 horse big-block and it handles all that power just fine. We started with a real strong case from a 4x4, but inside it's just the same as any heavy-duty 350 transmission. We used the aluminum lower torque converter cover instead of the tin one because that adds a lot of strength to the case, and we ran the factory braces from the engine back to the transmission. Those are things that anyone can do.

The 400 isn't a bad design, but it's bigger and it's longer so I figure if the 350 will do the job, why not use it? A rodder with a really killer motor might

John Sevelius explains that the 700 R4 needs this throttle cable to determine shift points and quality, while the 350 uses a vacuum line connected to the modulator.

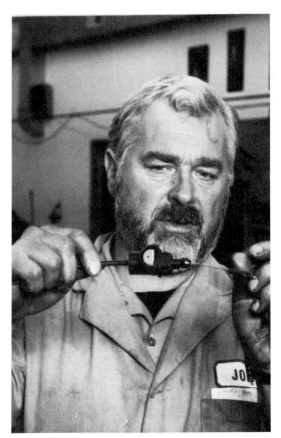

John points out the little brass button. Adjustments are made by pressing down on the button while someone inside the car holds the pedal to the metal.

need to run a 400, but most of the stuff on the street will work just fine with a 350.

Q: *What about the newer 700 R4 transmission? Is it a good choice for street rodders, and will it handle some extra horsepower?*

John: The 700 R4 is a great tranny for a street rod. It's a true four-speed, so you get a nice low first gear for good acceleration and an overdrive fourth gear that works great on the highway. Not all R4s are the same, however. The first four years, 1982 to 1986, weren't as strong as the later transmissions—but the earlier ones can be updated without any trouble.

Q: *These transmissions are designed to be controlled by the computer, right? What about rods without a computer; how do you control the transmission operation, and what about controlling the lock-up of the torque converter?*

John: If you don't have the computer, then you can buy a kit from Ron Francis [and other manufacturers as well] that takes over the computer functions. You can let that box control the converter lock-up. Some people hook up a separate switch for the lock-up control, but that can be kind of a pain. If you don't remember to unlock the converter when you slow down it will kill the motor, just like a standard transmission if you don't step on the clutch.

Q: *What about some other transmissions that a street rodder might want to run, some examples from other brands, and some good and bad choices?*

John: Well, in the GM line there's the 200 series automatics from the early 1980s. These weren't much good; a guy should just stay away from those. In the Ford line the C4 and C6 are both good; the C6 is stronger, of course. And then there's the 727 Torqueflite from Chrysler.

Q: *The 727 Torqueflite has a reputation as a real good transmission. What do you think?*

John: Oh yes, that's the one, the best one of all the automatics. It's simple, easy to repair, and absolutely bulletproof. I took one out of a 4x4 once with over a hundred thousand miles on it and you could still read the part numbers on the fiber clutches. It's one hell of a transmission!

A nice, simple rear transmission mount, formed from mild steel tubing and a pair of flanges.

The boss on the rear of a 350 can be used to check the
angle of the engine and transmission.

122

Chapter 6

Selecting and Installing the Rear Axle

Deciding which rear end and suspension to run under your rod is a tough choice. Much like choosing the engine, you need to consider how much money you want to spend and how the car will be used. The rear end and suspension must fit the overall plan for the car, be it a retro-coupe or pro-street sedan. In this chapter I have listed the most popular rear ends used in rods, along with some rear end and suspension installation information borrowed from the first book in this series, Boyd Coddington's How To Build Hot Rod Chassis.

How Many Bolts, How Many Inches?
The most popular rear end used in hot rodding today is no doubt the 9in Ford assembly. Consequently, a large part of this chapter is dedicated to that venerable axle assembly. But what if you can't find a 9in, or it's too expensive, or whatever? What else is available in the way of a good rear end for your old coupe?

A short and incomplete list of the alternatives would start with the 8in Ford rear end used in many mid-size Ford products. Though not as durable as the nine-incher, this is a perfectly

A vast variety of rear ends are available for your street rod, although some are better choices than others.

These axles are for a GM ten-bolt rear end. The stock roller bearings have been replaced by heavy-duty assemblies. In addition to being a better bearing, these assemblies keep the wheel attached to the car in case of axle breakage.

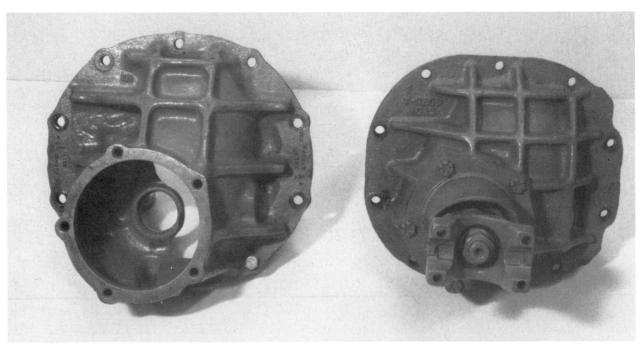

On the left is a 9in Ford housing and on the right is the slightly smaller 8in housing. Both are third-member designs, meaning the whole assembly with the ring and pinion can be pulled out of the housing for repair.

Ford axles for the nine-incher come in two diameters and two spline counts, thirty-one (stronger) or twenty-eight. The strongest combination is a large axle in thirty-one splines.

The most common bearing on a Ford axle is this tapered roller–although it can be replaced with a more conventional sealed roller bearing.

Ford 9in housings come with large or small diameter axles and bearings. The large axles use a larger bearing, as shown. The ID (inside diameter) of this housing is 3.15in while the smaller axle has a housing ID of 2.89in.

Some owners of light street rods run a mini-spool as an inexpensive replacement for a positraction unit. The spool eliminates the side and spider gears and locks the rear end.

A 9in rear end with factory disc brakes ready to be mounted in a new street rod frame.

good rear end and is a third-member design, meaning you can drop the center section out of the car and work on it while it's on the bench. Some of these Ford rear ends are only 56in wide, flange to flange, which means they fit many Deuces and later street rods without narrowing. Some of them came with factory disc brakes, another nice feature.

In the GM line the smaller, ten-bolt rear end used in many Chevy Novas and similar models is popular, though most of these rear ends measure over 60in from flange to flange. These rear ends are difficult to narrow, too, because the axle is tapered behind the splined area. A better choice is the rear end assembly from a mid-1960s Nova measuring only 57in from flange to flange. It's a convenient size, but also fairly hard to find.

The twelve-bolt GM rear end is stronger than the ten-bolt by about 25 percent, although it measures over 60in from flange to flange.

With the possible exception of the narrow ten-bolt units, the GM assemblies make a less than ideal rear end for a street rod. Because the axles are tapered behind the splines, they can't be cut and resplined. This means that you have to buy axles when you narrow a housing. GM rear ends are not a third-member design, either. Positraction units are hard to find for these rear ends as well, and they're expensive to buy when you do find them. Another thing, even a good twelve-bolt rear end isn't nearly as strong as either a 9in Ford or the 8 3/4in Mopar rear end.

The Mopar rear end can be a good alternative for a street rod. The design is strong and the units are often rather inexpensive (no one seems to want that old Mopar stuff). Some relatively narrow assemblies measuring 57in were used in Dodge Darts and Plymouth Dusters equipped with the 340 or 383ci engines in the late 1960s and early 1970s. These are a good choice for a street rod, but they can be hard to locate.

The axles in these rear ends are tapered behind the splines, so they can't be cut and resplined. This means that you will have to buy new axles when the housing is narrowed. The good news is that the Mopar rear end is a third-member design, and it shouldn't be too hard to find since Chrysler used a lot of deep gear sets and posi units. The other good news is that the basic design is strong—the Mopar rear end uses a stout housing and good strong gears.

Short Discourse on the Nine-Inch Ford Rear End

Why the Nine-Inch Ford?

You're building a new street rod and you wonder if, in fact, the 9in Ford rear end is the best one for the job.

The 9in Ford is very popular and the reasons are simple: It's strong, parts are readily available (both new and used), it's relatively easy to narrow, and it uses the "pumpkin" design with a removable center section (also known as a third-member design).

The nine-incher gets its strength from both a strong housing and good, stout gears with good contact between those gears. The Ford housing (there are different models available) is generally stronger than either the 8 3/4in Mopar or the twelve-bolt GM housings.

Finding a nine-incher isn't too tough, either, since the design was used for thirty years. The first 9in Ford rear ends were used in passenger cars and trucks as far back as 1957. Although passenger cars used the rear end only until 1973, pickup trucks continued to use them until 1984, and full-size Ford vans used them right up through 1987.

The Ford rear end is easier to narrow (a necessity in most street rod applications) than some other types due to its short tapered section

This sturdy fixture makes it easy to locate the rear end at ride height before installing the rear suspension linkage.

*A simple pair of ladder bars. Note the multiple holes,
providing a great deal of adjustment.*

*Independent suspension offers better ride and handling
than a solid-axle design. This system is based on the
Corvette rear suspension.*

A pro-street rear suspension at Metal Fab. Note the simple, effective axle brackets and the multiple mounting points for the four bars.

Another nine-incher in a fat-fendered frame. Before mounting the suspension, the frame and axle assembly must be at ride height.

just behind the axle splines. The design of the third-member style rear end (a design feature shared with the Mopar and the smaller 8in Ford) means that you can drop out the center section—for maintenance work or to install another center section with a different ratio—in a matter of an hour instead of a full day.

If there is a down side to the 9in Ford design it might include the price and availability of used positraction units. Though thousands and thousands of these rear ends were manufactured, the demand for these units by street rodders, drag racers, off-roaders, and anyone else interested in a really tough rear end means that prices aren't always cheap. If you want positraction with your rear end, the availability goes down and the price goes up.

How to Tell a Nine-Incher from a Nine-Incher

The Ford nine-incher was offered in a variety of housings and with a variety of axle and bearing combinations. First, beware of imitations. Ford manufactured a 9 3/8in rear end, visually

quite similar to the 9in version. The trouble is, there are few parts available for this oddball rear end. You can tell that the rear end is a 9 3/8in if you can place a socket straight onto the housing stud at the seven o'clock position. The other visual difference is the top horizontal rib on the housing. If the rib turns sharply down at one end, it's the 9 3/8in rear end. (*Note:* A clever shop can easily modify the larger housing to accept a 9in center section.)

The 9in housings were offered in two basic styles with one variant. More than 90 percent of the housings seen at swap meets have a single vertical rib at the top of the housing. A stronger, two-rib design was used during the first few years of production, though these center sections are rather rare. More rare than the two-rib design is the nodular housing, made from extremely strong nodular iron. These housings feature a large N, cast into the housing itself.

Ford manufactured 9in rear ends with different axle diameters, different axle spline counts, and different size wheel bearings. It's a little confusing, but it goes like this: Axles came in 28 and

This is a three-bar as assembled by Metal Fab. Like a four-bar, the system needs a panhard rod to limit lateral movement of the axle.

31 splines, in two shaft diameters. The larger diameter axle uses a larger wheel bearing. Thus the larger axle/bearing combination is not interchangeable with small diameter/small bearing housings. A 31-spline axle is always the larger diameter shaft, but a 28-spline axle can be either the large or small diameter axle shaft.

Large diameter axle shafts with the larger bearings have an axle housing inside diameter, or ID (at the wheel end), of 3.150in. Small diameter axles with smaller bearings (the smaller diameter axles are always 28 splines) have a housing ID of 2.89in. The 31-spline design is 35 percent stronger (torsionally) than a 28-spline shaft cut on the same diameter axle. The added strength comes from the larger diameter at the spline and the increased number of splines.

Besides the two different sizes of axle bearings, there are different styles of bearings as well. One of the most common is the tapered roller bearing. This bearing is lubricated by rear end lube and features a seal on the outside of the bearing. New bearings of this style are easy to find and purchase. Special sealed bearings that will replace the tapered roller bearing are also available. Single-and double-row ball bearings were used by the factory as well. Some of these are sealed bearings and use a separate seal on the inside of the axle. Some trucks with 31-spline axles used a special, double-row ball bearing that is unique in size and expensive to replace.

Summers Brothers Incorporated, in Ontario, California, manufactures special axles and components for many types of rear ends, and makes a special wheel bearing that will allow you to run the large diameter Ford axles in a housing built for the smaller diameter bearings and axles.

Which Rear End Is for You?

Trying to decide which style of 9in rear end to look for is mostly a process of elimination. The narrowest of the 9in housings were used in some Ford Grenada models. Some of these (and the Lincoln Versailles) also had factory disc brakes, a nice touch. If you can find the Grenada housing (a large *if*) it may be narrow enough for some later street rods (most of these measured 61 or 62in from flange to flange). For most of us,

A set of ladder bars and a nine-incher on a frame at Boyd's. The panhard rod is much easier to hook up on a third-member type of rear end.

This greasy old Ford housing came out of a pickup truck. A long axle assembly like this is a good choice.

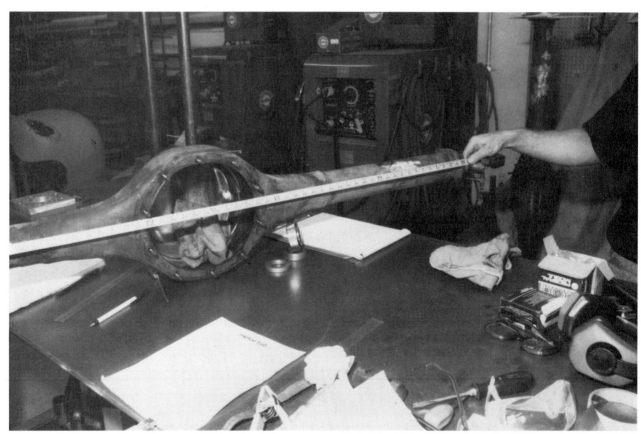

The rear end housing is measured carefully; in this case, both sides will be cut to leave the offset intact.

though, the nine-incher you buy from the bone yard will have to be narrowed.

If you can't find the narrow Grenada-Lincoln model, buy the widest 9in housing you can find (on a pickup truck or large passenger car). This way you are more likely to get a large, heavy housing and axles that are both large in diameter and long. Remember, there's a tapered area behind the splines with a smaller diameter. You want an axle with enough extra length so that when you cut it, you cut off all of the tapered section. The larger diameter axle will already be 31 splines, or at least big enough that it can be resplined from 28 to 31 splines.

Positraction for the Nine-Inch

Like the rear ends themselves, a variety of what we call "posi" units were offered for the Ford 9in design. The Equa-Loc and Traction-Loc are similar in design. Both were offered in two- and four-pinion designs, with four pinions being harder to find and much stronger. Both designs use clutch discs to control differential action. The Traction-Loc is the better of the two designs and

is available in both 28 and 31 splines. The Equa-Loc is available only for 28-spline axles.

More durable and more expensive is the Detroit Locker. This is a true locking differential with both wheels positively driven whenever the car is moving straight down the road.

A third option is available for full-time drag racing cars: the spool. In essence, the spool eliminates the spider gears and provides a rear end that's locked—all the time. Cheaper than even a used Equa-Loc, a spool or mini-spool can help the racer on a budget ensure that both tires receive equal power.

Narrowing a Rear End

The following procedure describes the narrowing of a 9in Ford rear end, although most of the steps would be the same for any type of rear end.

Before you can have that rear end narrowed, however, you need to measure just how narrow to make it. There are two ways to do this. The easiest way is to put the tires you intend to run on the rims you intend to use. With the car on jack stands at ride height, carefully locate the

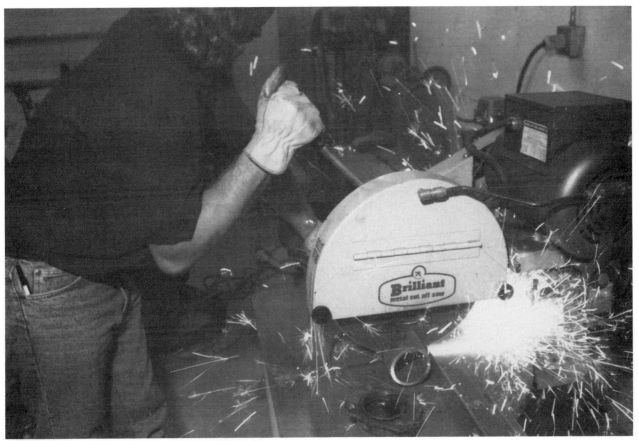

A cut-off saw such as this at Metal Fab makes short work (and neat work) of cutting the housing.

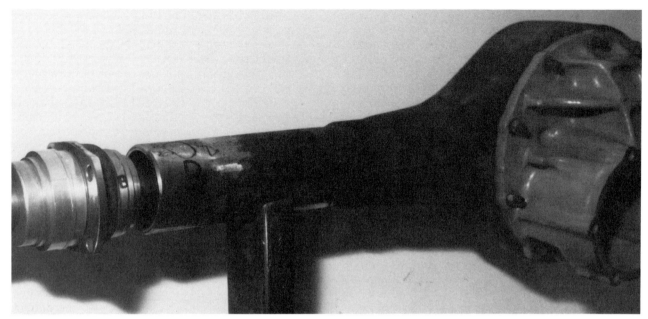

An alignment fixture must be used for final welding of the housing to eliminate any warpage caused by the heat.

The idea here is to install an 8in Ford rear end and new leaf springs in place of Henry's original rear end and buggy spring. The spring mounts have to be in-stalled per the instructions and also match up with the axle centerline.

tires where you want them to be. Once the tires are correctly located, raise and lower the car to ensure there is room for fender lips and suspension components.

As a rule of thumb, there should be at least 1in of clearance between the tire sidewall and the frame or leaf springs on the inside, and 1in between the tire and fender lip on the outside. With the tires blocked to sit exactly where you want them, measure carefully from the backside of one wheel to the backside of the other. This will give you the axle-flange-to-axle-flange distance.

The second way of measuring starts with the fender lip-to-fender lip distance. Subtract the clearance between the tire and fender times two, and subtract the front offset of each wheel times two. If it all sounds confusing, it is. Talk to the person or shop that is narrowing your rear end and measure it the way they want you to—with a sketch so everyone understands the measure-

ments. That way, there won't be any miscommunication.

Axles can't be cut and welded; they must be cut to the correct length and then resplined. If you are working with the larger diameter axles with 28 splines they can be resplined to 31 splines for more strength. This means, of course, that the 28-spline side gears will no longer work. In some cases it also means a little machine work because the hole in the ring gear carrier may be too small for the larger 31-spline axle.

The rear end housing itself is cut approximately 2in from the outer flange, so the area where the wheel bearing mounts is left intact. Then the correct amount of housing is cut off on each side to create the new, narrowed rear end housing. Usually, any offset from side to side is left intact, and equal amounts are removed from each side of the housing. In cases where you only need the rear end a little narrower, you can have just one side—the longer side—of the housing narrowed. (Make sure the new, narrowed rear end will put the driveshaft in the center of the

A simple piece of pipe can be used to mock-up the rear end installation. In the photo, the spring has been compressed to ride height and the amount of axle travel is checked. You need a minimum of 3in of travel before the axle hits the bumper.

Jim Petrykowski of Metal Fab likes to remind builders that the axle must be correctly located in all three planes.

driveshaft tunnel.) Before welding the end flanges back on, however, there's another step.

Welding the suspension brackets onto the housing will probably cause the housing to warp. Warped housings are very hard on wheel bearings and tires (and also quite common), so you should stop now, before having the end flanges welded onto the housing.

The idea is to temporarily bolt the axle housing and third-member into the car, correctly figure the U-joint angles, and then weld on the necessary suspension brackets or spring pads. After welding the brackets onto the housing, the axle housing itself should go back to the shop with the alignment fixture. Final welding of the axle housing ends should be done with the alignment fixture in place. That way, you know the axles and tires run absolutely true. When the brackets or pads are welded on *after* welding up the housing, the housing is often warped as a result.

So, if you can't find one of the rare Grenada-Lincoln rear ends, then buy the biggest one you can find. Plan to spend plenty of time (and possibly money) looking for a good used positraction unit. And follow all the steps I've already outlined when narrowing a rear end and welding on new saddle brackets.

Mounting the Rear End

Before mounting the rear end, you need to plan out the position of the axle and suspension. During this planning, remember that the wheelbase measurement isn't some kind of international standard. The goal is a rear tire mounted in the center of the fender opening—or at least where you want it mounted. The specifications sheet for a 1940 Ford lists the wheelbase as 112in. What they don't say is that most of the Ford products had the rear tire positioned near the front of the opening. As the car is lowered, the effect is exaggerated.

If possible, spend a little time mocking up the rear axle with wheels and tires to make sure the finished product will sit where you think it should. Ask the manufacturer of the rear suspension kit where their instructions will place the rear wheel and tire. Don't assume that there are

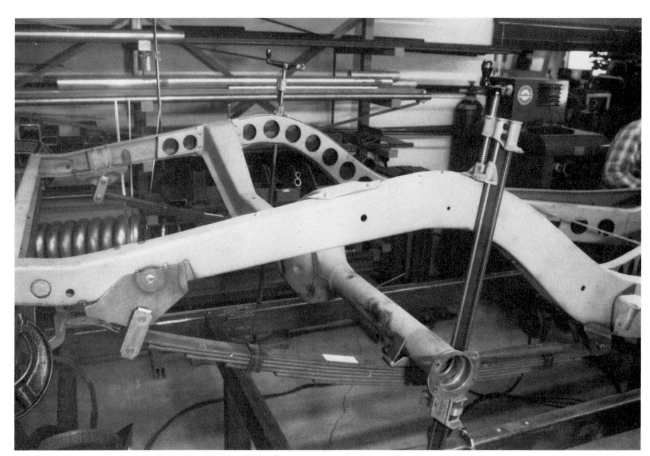

Installation is almost finished. The inside of the frame has been reinforced at the back, where the shackle brackets mount.

136

enough threads on the four bar adjusters to correct any mistakes in the position of the rear wheel and tire—figure it out ahead of time.

Rather than reinvent the wheel, I have reprinted part of the rear suspension chapter from the Boyd Coddington chassis book. It details the installation of a rear end with either leaf springs or four-bar rear suspension.

Mounting a Straight Axle with Leaf Springs

The first step in a situation like this is mounting the new leaf springs. A number of companies offer quality kits to convert Henry's buggy style cross-spring rear suspension to a pair of leaf springs. If you're building a rod from a Chevrolet product, and those old narrow rear leaf springs just aren't up to the task, new ones are available from a variety of suppliers. Open a catalog and order a new kit with improved springs and all the hardware needed to install new leaf springs under your Chevy (and most other brands as well). Many of these springs are already de-arched to keep the height nice and low, while offering a much stronger spring than those old originals.

When mounting a new set of springs, begin by setting the frame on a table of some sort. Position the frame at ride height and find the axle

Jim checks the pinion angle before the saddle brackets are welded on. The final measurement must be made at ride height.

137

centerline (fat Fords use an axle snubber that marks the centerline of the axle). After removing the old spring mounts where necessary, simply mount the spring perches per the locations that come with the new spring kits. Use a carpenter's square to ensure that the new perches end up with the mounting holes for the springs parallel to the ground (don't assume the sides of the rails are 90 degrees to the ground). You probably want to box the frame rails where the perches mount, or at least weld in a reinforcing tab to help support the weight where the spring perch mounts on the frame.

In order to simulate ride height or a load on the car, some builders put the springs in with only the main leaf, which makes it easier to load the suspension and see how everything really lines up. It also shows you how much clearance there is between the axle and the frame and where the tire will be positioned in the wheel-well.

You will have to run the suspension through full compression and rebound to correctly figure the shock mounting. In general, the shocks should use two-thirds of their movement on compression and one-third on rebound (starting from ride height). Most manufacturers suggest that shocks be mounted at up to 30 degrees from vertical, at ride height. Be sure to add axle snubbers that stop the axle movement on compression at least 1/2in before the shock absorbers bottom out. Don't use the shocks as the axle snubbers.

Once you have the suspension loaded—at ride height—you can determine the correct pinion angle and tack weld the spring saddles to the rear axle housing. It's a good idea to do the actual welding with a heli-arc to minimize the amount of heat transferred to the housing and reduce the chances for warpage.

Mounting a Four-Bar Rear Suspension

The kit featured here is from Pete and Jake's, and it's being installed in a Model A frame at the Metal Fab shop in Minneapolis. As always, you need to set up the frame on a level table and remember to work at ride height.

A finished installation. Saddle brackets were welded with a heli-arc for minimal heat buildup. Shocks and brackets are part of the complete spring kit.

138

Four-bar brackets like these on a Model A frame can be installed either first or last. You can mount the rear end on a fixture and work forward, or you can mount the brackets and work toward the rear.

There are two basic approaches when putting four-bars on the rear. If the kit gives dimensions for the location of the four-bar brackets, you can tack weld them on the frame, install the axle housing and the bars, and then see where everything ends up relative to the axle centerline already marked on the frame and table. Or, you can set the axle up under the frame, using a fixture of some kind to hold it correctly, and then just weld in the brackets wherever they end up on the frame rails (in the front-to-rear dimension).

In this case we chose to tack weld the brackets onto the frame first per the instruction sheet. Next, the rear end was mounted up under the frame using the axle centerline, ride height, and frame centerline as the references.

The frame brackets (no matter which method you use to locate them) need to be positioned so the bolt holes are level with the ground. Be sure the brackets are both the same distance from the ground, the same distance from the frame centerline, and the same distance from the axle centerline. These brackets need to be installed correctly—and they also need to be in exactly the same position on both sides. Small errors in the location of the mounting brackets are magnified and will require a lot of adjustment to correct later.

The pinion angle should be adjusted before the axle brackets are welded to the rear axle. Use a protractor and set the angle per the illustrations and notes in chapter 7. By setting the pinion angle before welding on the axle brackets we again save the threaded adjusters for use later.

The location of the four-bar brackets is checked against a frame reference point.

After setting the pinion angle, tack weld on the axle brackets, install the four bars, and see how everything stacks up. Check the rear axle position against the front axle centerline and the frame centerline, then double-check the pinion angle (remember, you are working in three dimensions, not just two). The four-bars should end up adjusted so that most of the threads are screwed into the rod and only a few threads are showing. Ideally, each bar has roughly the same number of threads showing.

By moving the axle up and down through full suspension movement, you can check for any binding in the linkage and determine the dimensions for the shock absorbers. You need two-thirds of the movement on compression and one-third on rebound. Don't let the shock act as the axle stop on compression or those expensive coilovers won't last very long. Always install the upper shock brackets after the axle has been adjusted for pinion angle, and keep the upper and lower shock mounts parallel.

The only thing left is the panhard rod, and that installation will vary slightly depending on the car and the individual kit.

Final welding can be done after all the dimensions have been checked one more time. Again, when the brackets are welded onto the rear axle, it's a good idea to do so with a heli-arc as this creates less heat and less chance of warping the rear end housing.

Conclusion

This business of rear ends and suspension systems might seem confusing at first. If there

The axle position is checked against the centerline and the distance forward to the four-bar brackets. It's a good idea to tack weld and then double-check all the dimensions before you do the final welding of the brackets.

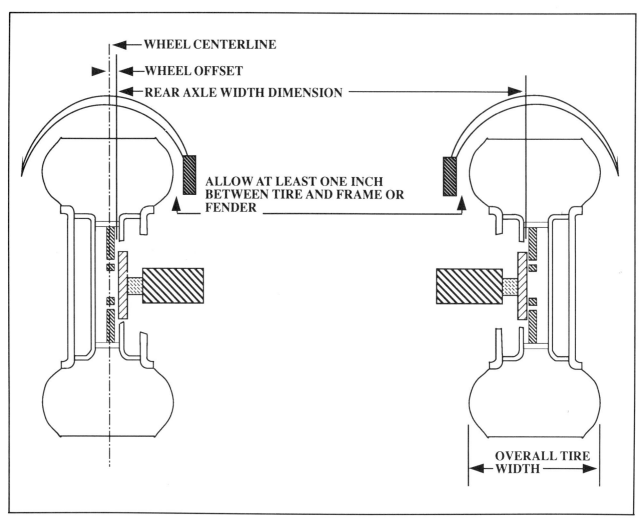

WHEEL CENTERLINE

WHEEL OFFSET

REAR AXLE WIDTH DIMENSION

ALLOW AT LEAST ONE INCH
BETWEEN TIRE AND FRAME OR
FENDER

OVERALL TIRE WIDTH

A sketch like this will help avoid confusion and ensure that you get the tire, wheel, and rear end dimensions that you need. If you are having a rear end cut to fit, mount the tires on the rims (if possible), set the rims up under the fenders, and measure from mounting flange to mounting flange. If you already have the rear end, *then use published width figures for your new tires plus the rear end dimension to determine where the tires will end up without any offset. Use rim offset (the difference between the mounting surface and the center of the rim) to place the tires where you need them in the wheelwell.*

seem to be too many options, then go back to your basic plan (you *do* have a plan for the car, right?).

Do you have a heavy foot that will be connected to a healthy engine? If not, you won't need the strongest rear end that's available and you won't need a positraction unit. You will need a rear end in good condition, one that doesn't leak (replace the seals before installing the new rear end). And you will need good brakes, so buy new shoes or disc brake pads now. Remember that sitting is hard on hydraulic components, so the wheel cylinders or calipers that came with the rear end probably need to be overhauled or replaced as well.

Do it neat, do it right, and don't worry so much about sex appeal. Concentrate first on how it works, then worry about how it looks.

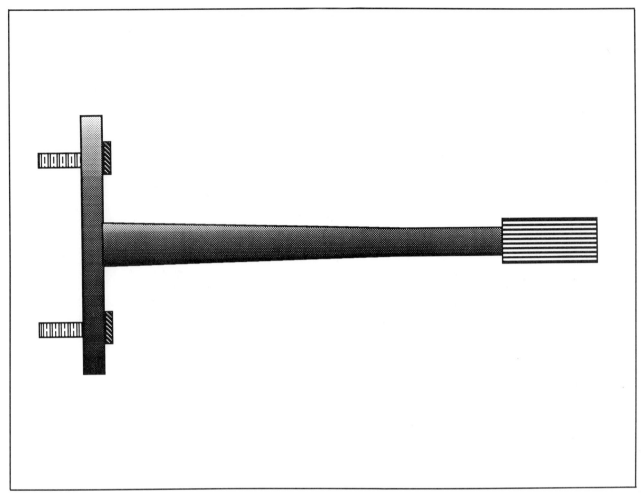

Many axles are shaped like this one, with a taper just behind the splined area. The tapered area is such a small diameter that you can't have new splines cut after shortening the axle. Ford has a relatively short ta-pered area and the axles can often be cut short and then resplined. Chrysler and GM have long tapered areas, meaning you will most likely have to buy new axles to fit the narrowed housing.

Chapter 7

Installing the Engine and Drivetrain

You may already understand how important the positioning of the engine is, but I'm going to re-state the case anyway: Street rodders, in particular, must pay close attention to engine placement. Some of these cars have extremely short engine compartments, and many builders place the engine very low in the chassis. While this may create a low center of gravity, it also puts the water pump snout pretty low in relation to the radiator. The water pump snout is, of course,

A small-block is being positioned in a frame at Boyd's. The engine has a water pump and fan in place.

the mounting point for the belt-driven fan. If the water pump and thus the fan end up too low in the frame, then you can only run a very small-diameter fan.

A good solution is to pay particular attention to engine position when you're building the car. Make sure the engine is high enough and set back far enough to make room for the fan, radiator, condenser, and shroud.

Planning

Installing the engine probably seems too simple to require any planning. Before just jamming the motor in place, however, consider that engine position affects the position of everything else such as the radiator, shroud, fan, condenser—the

list goes on. This is a case where you need to measure twice and cut once because if you do it wrong, it takes a lot of work to correct your mistakes.

The Boyd Coddington chassis book in this series covers the importance of sketching out the entire chassis before buying or bolting on any parts. The same applies here. You should know where the engine will sit, in all three dimensions, and where that puts all the other related components.

Usually, farther back is better, as it moves more of the weight toward the rear of the car. It also allows more room for an adequate radiator and, for cars with air conditioning, the condenser. Although you probably won't achieve a

Another Chevy small-block engine. Note the way the square tubing is used to check that the engine is level from side to side. First-time builders should mock-up *the radiator and front sheet metal so the radiator-fan relationship is sure to be right.*

145

fifty-fifty weight distribution without going to an Altered style engine location, moving the engine back as little as 2 or 3in can make a big difference in weight distribution.

Jack Chisenhall, owner of Vintage Air, located in San Antonio, Texas, encourages builders to mock-up the engine position with a fan on the engine and the radiator and front sheet metal in place. Jack comments: "Sometimes if these guys would just take a little notch out of the firewall they could move the engine back a few inches— enough to get the room they need for the right radiator, shroud, and condenser. Enough room so the final product is a 'real car,' one the owner can drive anywhere and anytime, because it doesn't overheat and the air conditioning works great."

The engine should be centered in the frame, between the two side rails. Though Detroit often offsets the engine slightly to the right, that probably isn't a good idea for your street rod. Detroit

does it to compensate for the weight of the driver, and to make room for the steering. Street rodders will do better to keep the engine centered in the frame, without any compensation or offset to one side.

The engine is the single heaviest part of the car. In order to keep a nice low center of gravity and make your street rod go around corners like a Porsche, you might want to get all that weight nice and low in the frame. That concept is sound, though you have to remember that the bottom of the oil pan is one of the most vulnerable parts of your street rod. In the end, it's kind of like a Limbo contest—you can only go so low! Five inches is a good minimum distance between the oil pan and the ground.

Jim Petrykowski, long-time street rod builder and owner of Metal Fab in Minneapolis, comments on the height of the engine in the chassis: "A lot of these cars have the through-bolt

These simple mounts transmit more vibration than a stock mount, but they are very strong. The small rack

underneath supports the engine while the mounts are welded in place.

on the motor mount [GM style mount] only about 1in higher than the top of the frame rail. Besides moving the belt-driven fan way down on the radiator where it doesn't move much air, it leaves the headers and the oil pan hanging pretty low–down where they're more likely to get caught on bumps in the road.

"By having the motor mount through-bolt positioned 3 to 4in above the frame rail, the engine is high enough that everything clears and you can run a decent sized, belt-driven cooling fan."

Once you've decided on a position for the engine, you need to think about the mounts themselves. Nearly all modern engines are mounted to the frame by three engine mounts. The two front mounts handle the bulk of the weight and also handle the enormous torque generated by a modern V-8. They told us in school that for every action there is an opposite reaction. The 300 horses and 400lb-ft of torque that are generated on a hard launch are transmitted to and through the chassis by only three points—so they had better be good ones.

In particular, consider the structural integrity of the mount design. Triangles are good, especially if they're made from strong tubular steel. Flat plate that comes out from the rails to meet the engine, without any supporting members, isn't so good.

Buying or Making Engine Mounts

In days of old, it was often necessary to make or modify your engine mounts. Today, a variety of mounts and mount kits are available. For both large- and small-block Chevy engines factory style mount kits can be ordered, or you can order mounts that use a single bolt through a urethane bushing.

The simple, factory style pad mount offers good isolation from vibration and ready availability. The triangular street rod mounts that utilize the urethane bushing allow very little flex and thus transmit more vibration to the chassis (and to the car's occupants). These mounts allow so little flex that the engine becomes an "almost stressed member" of the chassis.

The engine position must leave room for a good radiator and fan shroud. Both radiator and shroud are from Walker.

The fan shroud after being cut out and modified to fit the Ford radiator. A shroud will increase the efficiency of the radiator and cooling system dramatically.

When buying or building a rear mount, remember that the transmission may need to come out at a later date so be sure to provide a means for the cross-member or part of it to be unbolted and dropped out of the way. The rear mount itself should probably be a factory style mount.

Installing the Engine and Transmission

The job of setting the engine and transmission in the frame and mounting it correctly is made much easier with a small rack. The rack can be a fairly simple affair, just strong enough to hold the engine and transmission up off the table. By making it a little short, blocks and shims can be used to do the final positioning for engine height and angle. Without the rack or en-

The multi-blade fan pulls air through the center of the radiator (a shroud would help to move even more air). The air also must be able to move through the radiator and out of the engine compartment.

gine stand, you'll be wrestling with an engine dangling on a chain, trying to figure the location and the angle of the dangle–all while trying to keep the engine from moving.

A good way to check the height of the engine and to make sure it's the same from one side to another, is to run a piece of square tubing across the frame rails and then put two bolts into two of the holes for the front timing cover or water pump.

You should bolt on a water pump and fan (if you're using a belt-driven fan) before deciding on the final location for the engine. It's a good double-check of engine location and the available room between the water pump, fan, and radiator.

As stated before, you need at least 5in of clearance between the bottom of the oil pan and terra firma. If you are setting the engine and transmission into a bare frame, you need to know the location of the firewall. You probably will want to set the engine as far back as the firewall will allow. The engine should be set in the center of the rails, at the height you've determined to be correct.

When it comes to the correct angle for the engine, most shops dip the engine down at the back by one or two degrees. Some builders like to mount the intake manifold and then put a level across the carburetor mounting base to ensure that the engine is mounted so the carburetor is level or nearly level. The next question is, What about the driveline angles?

Figuring the Angle of the Dangle

Before determining the location of the rear end relative to the engine and the U-joint angles, it will pay to back up a little and talk about the joints themselves.

Most U-joints are designed to work in a range of five to ten degrees from straight and level, with the ideal being closer to five than ten. Remember that under acceleration, the U-joint angles (especially the rear-joint's) will change. The amount of change will vary according to the rear suspension design. Builders sometimes get in trouble by using a U-joint and yoke combination that doesn't provide much clearance between the U-joint cap and the yoke. If the installation of the rear end and suspension allows the angle to get fairly steep under acceleration or deceleration, the cap may contact the yoke. What's breaking U-joints in these cases is a design problem, not too much horsepower or too weak a U-joint.

If you are building a driveshaft of your own, be sure to keep the U-joints in phase. Driveshafts are commonly measured with the front yoke moved back 3/4in from the bottomed position. The actual measurement is from the center of

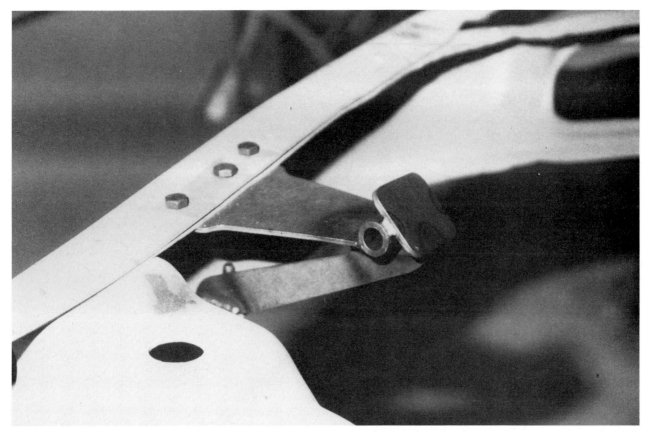

This simple bracket from Pete and Jake's is a strong, triangulated design and uses a factory style motor mount.

Somewhat higher on the evolutionary ladder, this billet bracket and mount is simple and very strong.

Variations on a theme: another billet mount with the single urethane bushing.

one cap to the center of the other. Whether you build your own driveshaft or have one built, be sure to spend the bucks and have the finished product balanced at a shop that specializes in driveshaft work.

Getting the Angles Right

A good way to start an argument among a group of street rodders is to ask each rodder how to correctly set the driveline angles. Even among professionals, there are some very different opinions. Some say the pinion angle (the angle of the centerline of the pinion shaft as seen from a side view) should match the angle of the engine and transmission, while others insist that the two angles should differ by at least one or two degrees.

Jim Petrykowski, a man who builds everything from very short wheelbase Anglias to large and long, fat-fendered Fords, feels that the only time the angles should be the same is in the case of short-wheelbase cars with gobs of horsepower. Professional shops have a long, telescoping steel rod that can be bolted onto the engine's main bearing caps and the rear end housing. When

When the car is designed to run in the weeds, the motor must be set up a little higher in the frame.

150

setting up a dragster chassis or serious pro-street Anglia, that special rod is used as a means of putting everything in one straight line so it can efficiently transfer enormous amounts or horsepower and torque.

In the case of more common street cars and street rods, the engine centerline is usually at a different height than the pinion. Jim likes to see a difference of one or two degrees between the angle of the engine and transmission, and the angle of the pinion (in side view).

As already mentioned, in the top view, the rear end often has an offset to one side. Jim usually leaves this offset intact, assuming that the dimensions of the finished rear end housing will place the driveshaft in the center of the driveshaft tunnel. In the top view, then, the centerline of the pinion and the engine are parallel, though they may be offset slightly.

In the side view, Jim prefers to work with a driveshaft in place. After years of building cars, he feels that the angle between the pinion and the driveshaft is the most important: "When I can, I just put a driveshaft in place between the engine and the rear end and then move the rear end housing until I have the pinion at the same angle as the driveshaft—and then I point the pinion down another one or two degrees."

When there is no driveshaft to mount between the transmission and rear end, Jim sets the pinion angle at the same angle as the engine—minus one or two degrees (with the nose pointed downward). The idea is to make the U-joints "work" as they rotate. If everything were in perfect alignment, the cross shaft would always rest against the same needle bearings in the cap. When the angles are different by a few degrees the cross shaft will walk around the caps, rotating the needles and spreading the load and wear. A difference of a degree or two is also a good way to dampen vibration and harmonics that can build in the driveline and resonate through the car.

Measuring Those Angles

Measuring the shaft angles can best be done with a simple protractor. While some transmission and rear end cases have areas where a good

Note how high the motor mounts are on this car (Dennis Varni's roadster at an early stage of construction) and the unusual front suspension.

*More hot rod than street rod, this car has an unusual
means of supporting the engine.*

A Hawk aluminum engine is dropped into Dennis Varni's roadster. The long engine support with the chains at either end features a threaded rod so the eyelet can be shifted backward or forward.

The engine is supported by a cradle across the front. This is a competition engine—production engines *should always be supported at the factory mounting points.*

measurement can be made, the most accurate readings are made across the yoke itself or across the caps of the U-joints.

Conclusion

When you're all finished, you should have an engine placed back far enough to allow room for good cooling system components and good airflow. It should be positioned so the belt-driven fan will pull air through the center of the radiator. The rear end should mount so that the pinion angle is slightly different than the angle of the engine centerline.

The rear end should have at least 3in of travel before it hits the compression stops, and there should be 1in of clearance between the tires and wheels and the suspension components or inner fender lip.

The best part about completing drivetrain installation is that now the chassis is nearly finished, and this project is finally starting to look like a car. The only things left are a little body and paint work, and work on the interior. Shouldn't take more than another couple of weeks, right?

Dennis and Boyd look satisfied with the finished installation—and well they should.

*Engine and transmission angle can usually be checked
at some convenient point on the transmission case, or
you can measure across the U-joint yoke.*

*Most shops run the pinion angle at one or two degrees
less than the angle of the engine.*

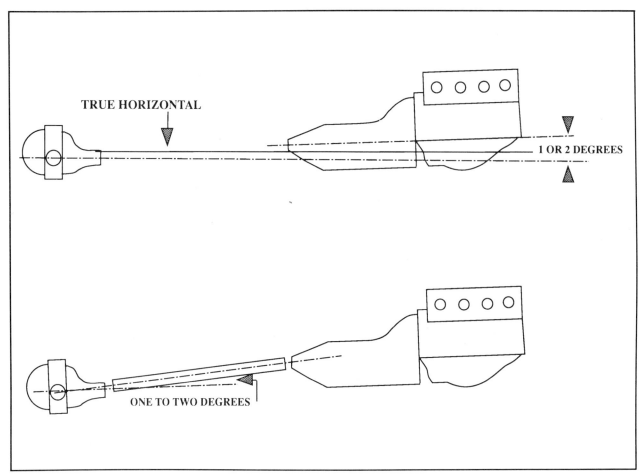

TRUE HORIZONTAL

1 OR 2 DEGREES

ONE TO TWO DEGREES

When there is no driveshaft to install, the pinion angle can be adjusted (top) to point down 1-2 degrees more than the engine centerline—at ride height, of course. Not everyone will agree, but this setup (bottom) works.

Mount the engine where it needs to be (so the carb is level or the rear isn't lower by more than 2 degrees). Then mount a driveshaft and adjust the pinion angle to be 1 or 2 degrees different than the driveshaft angle.

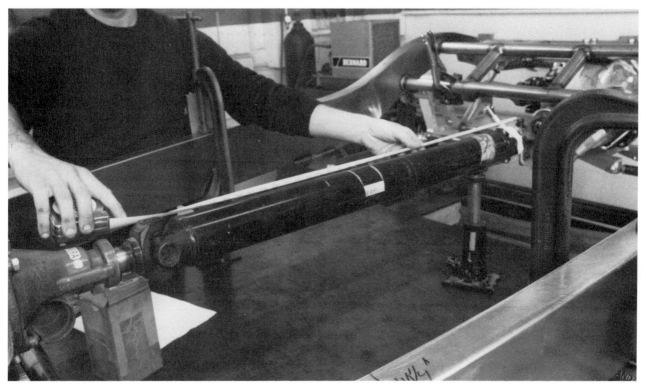

Driveshafts should be measured from the center of one cap to the center of the cap on the other end—with the
rear end at ride height and the front yoke pulled back 3/4in from the full-ahead position.

Another engine is lowered into place at Metal Fab. Note the simple, but effective hoist bracket and the rack under the engine.

Sources

Accel/Digital Fuel Injection
175 N. Branford Rd.
Branford, CT 06405

Arizona Speed and Marine
4221 E. Raymond St., #100
Phoenix, AZ 85040

Anoka-Ramsey Sports Center
Dyno Services
6760 Hwy. 10 N.W.
Ramsey, MN 55303

CARS
Attn: Art Chrisman
214 E. Alton
Santa Ana, CA 92707

Edelbrock Corporation
2700 California St.
Torrance, CA 90509

Ford Motorsport
Ford Motor Company
17000 Southfield Rd.
Allen Park, MI 48101

Metal Fab
1453 91st Ave. N.E.
Blaine, MN 55434
Attn.: Jim Petrykowski

Metro Transmission
John Sevelius
4030 Hoffman Road
White Bear Lake, MN 55110

Mopar Performance/Direct Connection
26311 Lawrence Ave.
Center Line, MI 48015-9760

Polar Chevrolet
1801 E. Co. Rd. F
White Bear Lake, MN 55110

R&R Performance
8420 Sunset Rd.
Spring Lake Park, MN 55432
(Dyno facility)

RDS Specialties Incorporated
R.R. 2, Box 177
LeSueur, MN 56058

Street and Performance
Rt. 5, #1, Hot Rod Lane
Mena, AR 71953

TPIS
4255 Co. Rd. 10
Chaska, MN 55318

Wheeler Racing Engines
10500 Nasau St.
Blaine, MN 55434

Index

Boyd Coddington's How to Build Hot Rod Engines and Drivelines is the second in a four-part series of Boyd Coddington Hot Rod How To books. If you have enjoyed this book, other titles from Motorbooks International include:

Boyd Coddington's How to Build Hot Rod Chassis, by Timothy Remus

Hot Rods by Boyd Coddington, by Timothy Remus

Hot Rods by Pete and Jake, by Pete Chapouris, Jim "Jake" Jacobs and Tony Thacker

Hot Rod Detailing, by Timothy Remus

Heroes of Hot Rodding, by David Fetherston

Motorbooks International titles are available
through quality bookstores everywhere.
For a free catalog, write or call
Motorbooks International
P.O. Box 1
Osceola, WI 54020
1-800-826-6600